"Mealtimes and bedtimes don't have to be stress_____ ___ __ Anne Meeker Miller's new book, *Mealtime and Bedtime Sing & Sign*. Her magical combination of music, sign language, and play can help parents and babies bring closeness, connection, and fun into these important times of day. Not to mention the tremendous benefits for communication—which makes for happier and more confident children, and provides a solid foundation for literacy. Happy singing and signing!"
—LAWRENCE J. COHEN, PH.D., AUTHOR OF *PLAYFUL PARENTING*

"We know now that the first days, months, and years of a child's life are a time of incredible learning. Children who have rich language experiences and positive interactions with others from birth develop important language and pre-reading skills that will benefit them for a lifetime. Anne Meeker Miller's *Mealtime and Bedtime Sing & Sign* is a truly joyous book that is beautifully constructed. This visually appealing resource of vocabulary and thematically conceived songs has my most enthusiastic endorsement!"
—DEE HANSEN, ED.D., AUTHOR OF
THE MUSIC AND LITERACY CONNECTION

"I love *Mealtime and Bedtime Sing & Sign*! The author's sense of humor shines throughout the book. Research has shown music and sign to be an effective means to foster language development and encourage early communication. The use of song and sign is also an enjoyable way to enhance the parent-child relationship. If I had a young child, I would be using this book every day."
—ALICE-ANN DARROW, PH.D., MT-BC, IRVIN COOPER PROFESSOR OF
MUSIC EDUCATION AND MUSIC THERAPY, FLORIDA STATE UNIVERSITY

"Our family loves Anne's music. My children responded immediately to the rhythm and words. The first time they listened to one of Anne's CDs, they got up and started acting out the songs all on their own. The music just seems to resonate with them. It's clear to me how important music and movement is to early communication. I witnessed it with my own children. *Mealtime and Bedtime Sing & Sign* should be a part of every family's library. Besides being educational, it's just plain fun!"
—JULIE BROSKI, AUTHOR OF *BEING ME*

"Imagine! Talking to an infant with your hands. *Mealtime and Bedtime Sing & Sign* will show you how to communicate with your baby through signs and songs. The baby is learning language and listening and motor skills as he or she bonds with you. Nurturing, playing, learning, and bonding together will lay the groundwork for a lifetime of learning and positive experiences. What could be better for baby?"

—JACKIE "MISS JACKIE" SILBERG, AUTHOR OF
LEARNING GAMES: EXPLORING THE SENSES THROUGH PLAY

"As a mother and a therapist, I highly recommend *Mealtime and Bedtime Sing & Sign* as a tool to support and enhance early communication and language development. It incorporates music, signing, and playing in promoting the development of motor, cognition, social-emotional, and language skills. As one who appreciates resources that are grounded and supported by research, I particularly liked the 'references and resources' section of the book, as it allows for further reading. My family thoroughly enjoys the music CD, and I appreciate the fun tunes with built-in repetition that support all kinds of learning. Thanks!"

—INGRID B.

"I have my Masters in Deaf Education and know sign language very well. I did not know if I would gain anything out of a sign language book for my son. The thing that is so great about this book is that it is more than just signing. I got inspired about singing and making up songs about everything and making simple home-made toys for him to play with. I would definitely recommend this program to anyone, whether they are new to sign language or already sign fluently."

—KELLY W.

"I am a pediatric dietitian and a mother of two, so I understand the many challenges associated with mealtime. *Mealtime and Bedtime Sing & Sign* is an excellent resource for parents to help make mealtime relaxed and fun for the entire family. Signing with your baby and toddler can help decrease mealtime stress and turn the dinner table from a battlefield to a rewarding family experience. I hope you enjoy communicating with your baby with sign language as much as I do!"

—CHRISSY S.

MEALTIME & BEDTIME SING & SIGN

ANNE MEEKER MILLER, PH.D.

MEALTIME & BEDTIME SING & SIGN

Simplify Your Child's Daily Routine
the Fun Way, through Music and Play

Da Capo
LIFE
LONG

A Member of Perseus Books Group, Inc.

Set in 12 point Perpetua by the Perseus Books Group

Library of Congress Cataloging-in-Publication Data

Miller, Anne Meeker.
    Mealtime and bedtime sing & sign : simplify your child's everyday routine the fun way,
through music and play / Anne Meeker Miller. — 1st Da Capo Press ed.
        p.   cm.
    Includes bibliographical references and index.
    ISBN 978-1-60094-021-7 (alk. paper)
    1. American Sign Language—Study and teaching (Early childhood) 2. Interpersonal
communication. 3. Deaf children—Means of communication. 4. Deaf children—
Language. I. Title. II. Title: Mealtime and bedtime sing and sign.
    HV2474.M539 2008
    419.7—dc22   2008014620

First Da Capo Press edition 2008

Published by Da Capo Press
A Member of the Perseus Books Group
www.dacapopress.com

Da Capo Press books are available at special discounts for bulk purchases
in the United States by corporations, institutions, and other organizations.
For more information, please contact the Special Markets Department at the
Perseus Books Group, 2300 Chestnut Street, Suite 200, Philadelphia, PA 19103, or call (800)
810-4145, ext. 5000, or e-mail special.markets@perseusbooks.com.

1 2 3 4 5 6 7 8 9

"And now," cried Max,
"Let the wild rumpus start!"

—*Where the Wild Things Are* by
Maurice Sendak (HARPERCOLLINS, 1963)

For my husband, Dan,
and sons, Andy, Kevin, and Greg:
Long may we "rumpus"!

CONTENTS

PREFACE

Language, especially how children learn their first language, has been a fascination of mine for years. Before I was married I earned undergraduate and graduate degrees in Linguistics. When I had my first baby, I saw a book about using sign language to help preverbal babies communicate. It provided delightful communication as well as a bonding experience with my firstborn; I followed the same simple process with subsequent children, teaching only a few key signed vocabulary words.

It would seem that by my fourth child, reading a *Baby Sing & Sign* book would be redundant. Nothing could be further from the truth. Being a busy homeschool mother, I appreciated time set aside to focus on the baby—who can easily get "lost" in our family of six. Furthermore, the older children were as captivated by the process as the baby, if not more so! And my baby boy loved all the attention he received from his older siblings as we sang and signed together.

Beyond the benefit of setting aside time for my youngest to interact with him on a one-on-one basis, I learned that there was a sensible and practical expansion of what I had done with the older children as I taught them to sign. I quickly added signs to our family repertoire and this became something that just fit into life—with no extra time or undue effort. The homemade toy ideas were excellent. Above all, the simple tunes and lyrics have become something of a new family tradition for us. If my youngest gets fussy or bored, a round of his favorite *Baby Sing & Sign* song changes everything!

Our family has benefited much from enjoying the *Sing & Sign* programs together.

—*Carol Webster*
Kansas City, Missouri

INTRODUCTION

Yes, there is a Nirvanah; it is leading your sheep
to a green pasture, and in putting your child to sleep,
and in writing the last line of your poem.

—KHALIL GIBRAN

Nothing is more satisfying for parents than meeting the needs of our babies.

When we first become acquainted with our newborn, she is not that complicated; she needs to be fed, clothed, and cuddled, and she sleeps away a good portion of her first months. I can relate to Shirley MacLaine's character in the movie *Terms of Endearment,* when she bounced her baby around in her crib to make certain she was breathing, and awakened her baby daughter in the process—I was so excited about bringing my infant son home from the hospital that I did my fair share of gently jostling him. I wanted him to realize in his own baby fashion that I was on duty and ready to roll at a moment's notice.

And oh, the pride we take in meeting the whims of our little ones. We throw ourselves into this job with the single-mindedness and determination of an athlete training for a triathlon. We give voice to every quivering chin and whimper or wail of displeasure: "You must want your diaper changed . . . Surely you are overly tired from your first visit to the zoo . . . I bet you are too warm from wearing your long-sleeved sleeper . . . You're cranky because you're teething!" It is human nature for parents to want to explain an infant's sadness or discomfort.

1

As our child grows, so does the list of possible issues causing her tears and frustration. She wants a specific snack or toy; she is terrified of brown dogs, but white and black ones are just fine; her yellow sundress is scratchy and uncomfortable; she wants to feed the ducks at the park now and not later! With such a long list of potential baby grievances, how do we resolve the problem if we are simply guessing at its origin?

The solution for many parents is to teach their hearing babies sign language so they can communicate their wants and needs. When you teach your baby key signs such as MORE, PLAY, EAT, DOGGIE, PLEASE, HELP, and MILK, you are giving her the opportunity to solve some of her own problems. Then she can let you know what she wants and you can respond consistently with the particular type of help she needs: provision of a snack, more snuggling on the couch, going outside to play with Scruffy the dog.

In my first book, *Baby Sing & Sign,* I introduced a sign language communication program that provides numerous developmental benefits for babies and enhances the lives of families with young children. Through music and play activities, parents can teach their infants key signs from American Sign Language (ASL), the language commonly used by the deaf community.

The method is an outgrowth of my work as a music therapist for a public school system in the Kansas City area. Several years ago a colleague asked me to explore the use of music as a way to help infants and toddlers learn to sign. I wrote or arranged some child-friendly songs with lyrics that focused on basic vocabulary words. These often-repeated words made sign language practice simple and fun. Music proved to be a powerful and motivating tool for teaching sign language. Not only were babies responsive, but both they and their parents were having fun!

Mealtime and Bedtime Sing & Sign tackles parenting challenges specific to feeding babies and making sure they get adequate rest. I apply the best practices in teaching babies and toddlers new skills by incorporating music, play activities, and rich picture book literature into our sign teaching. Over two hundred ASL signs are shared, along with hundreds of practical teaching tips and fun family activities. You'll be able to create a language-rich environment for your child in your own home, promoting deep learning of the essential vocabulary words babies and toddlers need to master communication with others.

I also share plenty of creative ways that parents have utilized sign language to help develop their baby's healthy eating and sleeping habits. My hands-on approach helps you create routines, redirect mealtime or bedtime meltdowns, and anticipate some of the parenting "potholes" that may lie ahead. Most importantly, I give you ideas for savoring each moment with your child as you snack, sup, snuggle, and sleep.

Avery signs DOWN.

WHY SIGN?

Babies can communicate their wants and needs using gestures long before their vocal mechanisms are mature enough to verbalize. In groundbreaking research, child psychologists Linda Acredolo and Susan Goodwyn found that using sign language with children at an early age supports the natural development of their ability to speak. Babies who learn to sign experience less frustration and often verbalize sooner than their peers, and most importantly, sign language strengthens the bond between caregiver and child. Acredolo and Goodwyn's "baby signs" are gestures they invented or modified from American Sign Language to best fit the hand-shape development of babies.

Teaching your hearing baby to sign is an extension of the types of nonverbal communication she already uses to get your attention: crying, facial expressions, gesturing, making noise, crawling toward an object she desires, and more. Most children create their own signs to tell you what they want and need, such as pointing to a desired object or waving their hands across their bodies with a grumpy look. Pointing at the pantry in search of a certain snack food may lack precision, and that grumpy arm wave gesture is likely to baffle you, as it can mean so many things in the same day: "I want my stuffed bunny right now," "I don't like peas so take them off my plate," or "I am trying to learn to crawl across the kitchen floor all by myself so quit trying to help me!" These types of "signs" are ambiguous and can often contribute to even more frustration for your child.

Some benefits of teaching babies and toddlers ASL-based signs include the following:

○ The ASL hand shapes often form "pictures" of the objects or ideas they represent and are therefore simple for the child to learn. For instance, the sign for EAT is performed by tapping gathered fingertips to the lips, pantomiming the act of eating food. Your child may learn to perform some of the signs quickly, improving your communication with one another in no time at all.

○ Many daycare centers are teaching ASL signs to children birth to two years of age. It then becomes easier for caregiver and parent to communicate with a child if they both use a commonly accepted sign language. Also, when a child needs to move from one daycare center to another, the transition is smoother because both centers are likely using an ASL-based approach.

○ Teaching basic vocabulary words in American Sign Language to your child at an early age may enable her to use these skills with toddler- or preschool-aged peers who are hearing impaired or deaf. Because siblings often continue to practice their signed words with their younger brothers and sisters, I find that many children starting preschool or elementary school know basic signs. The same words they use with the babies in their family will come in handy at play centers or on the playground: "Do you WANT to PLAY with me?"

You should always say the words to your baby as you teach her to sign; sign language is your tool to help your child learn to speak. Sign language builds a communication "bridge," supporting your baby's ability to receive and understand spoken words—and helping her tell you what she wants and needs—until that time when she can speak the words intelligibly.

Just as most babies stop crawling once they learn to walk, most will stop signing a word once they can speak it. Speaking is easier than signing for most children. Immersing your baby in words—spoken, signed, and sung—gives her more than one way to grasp their meaning as well as exposure to lots of different words, to supply her with all the enrichment and support she needs to learn to speak.

Some ASL signs are too difficult for baby fingers. For this reason, I have modified some of the signs so they are a better developmental fit for the fine motor skills of infants and toddlers. Children may modify a sign further and do their own version of that sign. These individualized gestures should be accepted and praised: "Great job signing

CRACKER, buddy. Here are some crackers for your snack." Parents should continue to model the signs as they are described in this book. With practice and time, babies and toddlers often become more precise in their signs. However, babies and toddlers don't need to sign with precision. All they need is a caring adult who will learn to interpret their child's gestures and respond in a consistent and encouraging way.

WHAT SCIENCE SAYS ABOUT SINGING AND SIGNING

For those who are interested in findings from the scientific community regarding infant and toddler language acquisition, here are a few excerpts from some notable research studies:

○ Michael Brent, Ph.D., researcher at Washington University in St. Louis, found that children younger than fifteen months learn words primarily spoken by their parents in isolation. For instance, when they hear single words such as "go," "carrot," or "mouse," they learn the words much easier than if they hear them in a longer sentence. The frequency with which the parent speaks a word is also a critical determinant of whether the child will know that word later. This finding supports the use of sign language because repetition and the practice of words in isolation are natural elements of the sign teaching process.

○ In her book, *What Kids Need: Today's Best Ideas for Nurturing, Teaching, and Protecting Young Children* (Beacon Press, 2002), parenting expert Rima Shore makes the important point that babies learn language in the context of their relationships with caring adults. She notes that by the time babies are nine months old, parents typically follow their child's line of vision to an object of interest and proceed to label the item for their baby: "That's a BUTTERFLY. Isn't it pretty? Look at its colorful wings." Says Rima, "This kind of responsiveness fosters infants' language acquisition." This interaction is possible only through "face time" with your child; educational DVDs cannot fulfill this important requirement.

○ Kathy Hirsh-Pasek, Ph.D., and Roberta Golinkoff, Ph.D., co-authors of *How Babies Talk: The Magic and Mystery of Language in the First Three Years of Life* (Plume, 2002), found that infants and toddlers learn language differently. Babies younger than twelve months learn the names of objects they are most interested in. Toddlers, however, pay more attention to social cues, and want to talk about what their parents are interested in. Parents should express interest in, label, and discuss objects that are of interest to their child. Says Golinkoff: "So when you're at McDonald's . . . [and] you're holding a french fry and talking about divorce, your baby might learn [that] the word 'divorce' goes with a french fry. Talking with children matters, even at this very early age."

THE *SING & SIGN* PROGRAM

Sing & Sign is a unique approach to teaching sign language and is ideal for busy families. The program uses music, simple play materials, games, and picture books to help you and your baby learn and practice a variety of easy and essential words from American Sign Language that can be used in meaningful communication. The original *Baby Sing & Sign* book and CD features upbeat songs for learning basic words and ASL. The proven benefits of music and sign language continue with *Toddler Sing & Sign*. Older toddlers and preschoolers learn to express themselves and learn more about the world, mastering signs for animals, colors, feelings, and more.

Thousands of families have successfully used *Baby Sing & Sign* to teach their infants to sign. *Mealtime and Bedtime Sing & Sign* is a new installment to this program built specifically to remedy challenges you encounter when feeding your baby and getting her to sleep. In addition to signing, your baby will enjoy the wonderful songs, games, and activities that fit effortlessly into your busy life with her. *Mealtime and Bedtime Sing & Sign* will help your child make important connections between the objects and events in her life and their labels.

♪ About the Mealtime and Bedtime Signs

The signs and words included in the book were chosen because of their importance for communicating with eating and sleepy babies. I've given you an extensive menu of vocabulary words for food choices and manners. The signs I have selected for bedtime include clothing and activities customary for "night-night" routines, as well as favorite people, activities, and animals that babies like to sing and read about before they climb into bed.

Mealtime and Bedtime Sing & Sign provides two photographs for each sign taught in the book. One shows an adult model performing the ASL sign of a word. The second photograph shows a child performing a modification that a baby or toddler might make when she attempts to perform that same sign. It is important to always look for the child's best attempt to sign the gesture and to respond with praise.

♪ About the Mealtime and Bedtime Songs

The twelve songs in this book and on the CD are arranged from start to finish with eating and sleeping babies in mind. The first five songs are all about food and mealtime; the next five songs are about bedtime rituals, gradually transitioning your child to her crib or bed. The two bonus songs at the end of the CD are lovely lullabies that you can play to your child as part of your bedtime routine to send her off to slumber.

Each song on the CD provides opportunities to sing as well as sign the vocabulary included in the book. Some songs were composed for the program; others are slightly modified or expanded versions of uncommon folk tunes. The melodies are simple but musically interesting to your baby—a child can recognize and respond to the tune and rhythm, and will delight in any new verses parents and caregivers may add to extend the fun and learning.

When *Mealtime and Bedtime Sing & Sign* is used as a language development program, I recommend singing the songs with babies for several weeks to provide repeated opportunities to hear and enjoy the music. The tunes make up a repertoire that can be enjoyed by the entire family. As with the first two *Sing & Sign* CDs, parents have shared with me that the benefit of including these songs in their family life has endured long after their children have learned to speak.

Here are a few more ideas for singing and signing with your baby:

- After you have listened to the CD and learned the tunes, *you can alternate singing with or without the CD.* Singing without musical accompaniment is called *a cappella* singing. Your a cappella singing will become a source of comfort and pleasure for your child, and will create opportunities for your baby and your entire family to devise their own games.
- *Musical creativity is strongly encouraged!* As you sing the songs without the CD, make up verses that will make your child smile and incorporate a variety of your child's signed vocabulary words in fresh and interesting ways. Babies especially like songs that include their name. For instance, try singing a variation of "John the Rabbit" that might go something like this: "Oh, Sam the baby had a mighty good habit of EATING all his carrots . . ." You can substitute any food or animal to create new verses for "My Kitchen Door."

- *Consider your child's developmental level and enjoyment of the song* when you choose which signs to include as you sing. The signing should not detract from the child's musical pleasure!

- *Emphasize only one word in a sentence.* Research studies have found children learn words best when they are taught one at a time. The sign directions in the songbook suggest one or two words per phrase for you to sign as you sing with your child. Older children may enjoy signing more than one word.

- *Embed the music in your daily activities* just as you do your sign language teaching and practice. Make music a natural extension of your routine. The songs are infinitely portable and don't require a CD player to enjoy. Simply sing and sign any of the *Mealtime and Bedtime* songs (or your favorite childhood tunes) as your child takes a walk, plays inside or outside, rides in the car, bathes, or cuddles.

- *Singing provides an important context for your child to sign.* The structure and predictability helps her recall the gestures and grasp the meaning of the words the sign represents. She might be willing to sign some of the key vocabulary words of the song, "White Sheep and Black Sheep" as you sing. However, asking her to "show Uncle Bob your SHEEP sign" may bewilder your child, because there are probably no sheep in Uncle Bob's living room. Signed words need a context that makes sense to your child. Music provides the "sign setting."

Maizie signs MORE

HOW TO USE THIS BOOK

Make sure to consume this book in small bites. There are over a thousand activities, resources, suggestions, and songs to help you teach more than two hundred signed vocabulary words. Take your time as you add signs and songs to your day-to-day family life. Before you begin teaching your child to sign, flip through the book from cover to cover. Thumb through the "*Mealtime and Bedtime* Dictionary" and mark the pages of words you would like to teach your child. *Key mealtime vocabulary words are marked with* ☀ *and important bedtime words are marked with* ☽ . *This can guide you in choosing a core vocabulary list if this is your first baby sign language experience.* You should also follow your child's lead in selecting signs that have meaning for her. If she adores her teddy bear, then BEAR should be one of the signs you teach first.

Start enjoying the music CD with your child as you drive in the car, prepare meals, play inside, or rock before bedtime. Once you are familiar with the tunes, you can begin to add your new signed vocabulary words as you listen and sing along. Each page in the "*Mealtime and Bedtime* Dictionary" includes a list of songs that you can sing to practice that specific signed vocabulary word.

Mealtime and Bedtime Sing & Sign is a process that allows you to capture your child's attention with music and teach sign language in such a playful way that children never realize they are learning new skills. The program is designed to enhance, rather than complicate, your child's and your daily routine. "Teaching Your Child to Sing and Sign" (page 13) outlines the basics for teaching children how to sign and illustrates the hand formations that will be used throughout the book. The "*Mealtime and Bedtime* Dictionary"—the centerpiece of the book—is an alphabetized presentation of more than two hundred signed words that are meaningful and practical for young children (page 23).

For each vocabulary word, I provide:

- ○ *A photograph of an adult model* performing the ASL sign and directions for how to perform it
- ○ *A photograph of a child model* performing the same sign, with suggestions for ways a child may modify it. Due to the limitations of little hands, it is difficult to perform some hand shapes and combinations of movements.
- ○ *Tips for teaching the sign* that are practical, playful, interactive, and fun!

○ *Songs to sing and sign* the vocabulary word. Music provides the perfect context for learning language and makes the repetition essential to mastering new vocabulary words easy and enjoyable.

○ *Signs of Success stories* from parents and caregivers who have participated in *Sing & Sign* on their own or in classes. They share practical advice about how to teach specific signs in the dictionary.

Throughout the "*Mealtime and Bedtime* Dictionary" you will find two other components of the program, *Sign Solutions* and *Play, Sign, and Learn*.

Sign Solutions. Here you will find practical information and advice specific to the types of mealtime and bedtime challenges parents often face. What can you do to help a picky eater expand her repertoire of food choices? How do you create a peaceful bedtime routine so that your baby doesn't fuss and cry when it is time for you to leave the room? With the guidance of a pediatrician and dietitian, you will learn how sign language can be an important tool in resolving eating and sleeping conflicts with your child.

Play, Sign, and Learn. For each word in the "*Mealtime and Bedtime* Dictionary," you will find play activities for teaching the new vocabulary word. Some play activities require assembling a few materials or sharing a broader set of fun ideas based on the theme the signed word provides. These *Play, Sign, and Learn* activities are full of great information or a fun activity for you and your child to enjoy at home while you teach specific vocabulary words.

Following the "*Mealtime and Bedtime* Dictionary" is the "*Mealtime and Bedtime* Songbook" (page 177). The songs follow the order of the playlist on the music CD (found inside the back cover). For each song, you will find:

● *A complete list of all the signed words* taught in this book that appear in the lyrics of the song.

● *A short story sharing the origin of the song.* The rhythm, rhyme, and repetition of each tune provide comfort and predictability for babies, but the instruments and musical imagery will maintain her interest. To capture the imagination and attention of adult listeners as well, I want you to know a little bit about the songs you will be singing over and over again with your babies.

● *Song lyrics complete with simple instructions for signing* the tune with babies, as well as suggestions for additional signs you could include if you use the song with older toddlers or preschoolers. When singing with babies, you should limit the number of vocabulary words you sign. However, some toddlers and preschoolers enjoy the challenge of signing more words than a baby would be able to accomplish.

● *Musical score with guitar chords* for those of you who would like to play along as you sing. However, these songs are meant to be enjoyed with or without accompaniment. Once you have listened to them several times, you are welcome to take them with you in your head and sing them with enthusiasm as you take a walk to the park or serenade your child during a car ride. Your child loves your singing best! No musical instruments are necessary other than your voice.

"A *Mealtime and Bedtime Sign & Sign* CD Index" is also provided (page 229). Each vocabulary word is listed, along with the songs that include that word in their lyrics. The index will help you quickly and easily find the signs you are teaching your child in their musical context on the CD.

For your convenience, *Sing & Sign* includes a master "*Mealtime and Bedtime* Pictorial Dictionary" containing all the signs used in the book (page 235). These pages can be duplicated so that you can keep a copy in your diaper bag or posted on your refrigerator door for quick reference. The "References and Resources" section lists books and Web sites about language development and music for young children (page 271).

Isaac signs EAT

A list of picture book recommendations is included in "Sing and Sign—and Read—with Picture Books" (page 247) for reading and signing the words in the "Pictorial Dictionary." The list can be duplicated so that you can take it with you to the library or book store; you can also share a copy with relatives looking for great birthday and holiday gift ideas for your child. Reading aloud to babies improves their listening skills and helps them understand the meaning of words. Reading books also increases the number of words a baby hears in a day. According to reading specialists Caroline Blakemore and Barbara Weston Ramirez, this is the single most important determinant of future school success (see "References and Resources," page 271).

Here are some organizational features used throughout the book. Vocabulary words to be signed appear in all capital letters. The pronouns "he" and "she" are used alternately to refer to babies and toddlers who will use the program. Safety reminders appear in **bold italics**. The book refers to both "parents" and "caregivers" when describing caring adults who will use the program with children. Given the growing diversity of families, feel free to modify the song texts and other activities as needed to fit your family structure.

A NOTE ON HOMEMADE TOYS

Throughout the "*Mealtime and Bedtime* Dictionary," I suggest games and other activities that reinforce the sign as well as creating homemade toys. When making and using homemade toys, the safety and well-being of your child are the first concerns. Please read the following points carefully before proceeding with any of the homemade toys described.

○ *Homemade toys have not been subject to mandatory toy safety regulations. Please use your best judgment when preparing and playing with these items.*
○ *Infants and toddlers must be supervised at all times when using toys.*
○ *Babies put things in their mouths. Be sure toys are too large for them to choke on, are nontoxic, and have smooth surfaces.*
○ *As with all toys, check toys often to be certain they are safe for play.*

TEACHING YOUR CHILD TO SIGN AND SIGN

TAKE THE TIME to peruse this book before you jump into sign language teaching if *Mealtime and Bedtime Sing & Sign* is your first child sign language program. In the meantime, introduce the music CD to your child and enjoy the tunes!

Think about the typical activities of your day together. Does your child have preferred toys, activities, foods, family members? Pick a set of five to six signed words to begin teaching to your child. Key words for mealtime ☀ and bedtime ☽ are marked with these sun and moon icons in the *Mealtime and Bedtime* Dictionary. I suggest you start with words such as EAT, PLAY, and MUSIC. They are broad enough and can be repeated many times during the child's day; there are always opportunities for baby to eat, play, and listen to music. Let your child direct you in selecting signs that have importance for him. Your child may adore carrots or his blanket, so be sure to include these words on his key signed vocabulary list. Start with what he cares about most.

STEP ONE: BABY IMITATES GESTURES

Do you remember how excited both you and your child were when he first waved "bye-bye" to Grandma or raised his hands above his head to show you he is "so big"? Chances are your child is already imitating your playful motions. Your first assignment as your child's sign language teacher is to help him imitate the gestures you make with your hands. By engaging his attention with your facial expressions and your speaking or singing voice, your child will watch you intently as you speak and sign to him. With lots of repetition and a caring adult who engages him in this Imitation Game as playfully as possible, your baby will likely copy your motions when he is ready.

You can help your child imitate the sign you are teaching by modeling it for him in two ways:

○ *Hand over hand.* Place your hands on top of the child's and gently shape the signs using his hands and fingers. He then learns what the signs feel like and figures out with practice that these motions are not random but are purposeful. Better still, he learns that your face is smiling and your voice is happy when he performs the desired hand motions.

○ *My turn, your turn.* When your child is able to look at your hands and then copy your motion with his own hands, he can plan his motor motions and improve the precision of his imitation skills. By watching you gesture and then taking a turn himself, he also learns that language is a reciprocal process; each person takes a turn. You can still use the "hand over hand" technique when you practice this turn-taking strategy. Praise him for taking a turn signing the word you are teaching or "talking with his hands."

Tate signs PLEASE.

STEP TWO:
BABY UNDERSTANDS SPOKEN
AND SIGNED WORDS

Before children can express their wants and desires using sign language, they must first understand the words and signs. The ability to receive and understand information is called receptive language. Anytime your child responds to your spoken words by looking at or reaching for the item you have requested, you are checking his receptive language skills. For instance, put a sippy-cup or a bottle of water on your child's high chair tray. Tell him, "Here is your WATER. Take a drink." Does he follow this simple direction? When you read a book together and ask him, "Where is the RABBIT in the picture?" does he look at the bunny or touch it with his finger? Give him several toys and ask him to hand you the BALL, the DOG, the BEAR. Does he hand you the toy you request? Practice these types of simple receptive language tasks with your baby. His responses to your questions or request may be subtle: a glance at the object you discuss, a raised eyebrow, a startled look, a smile. What words does your child understand?

After your child can imitate your motions and understands your spoken words, he must learn the connection between the gesture and the meaning of the word itself. Your baby may believe you are praising him because he looks adorable when he taps his chin. He doesn't realize that he is signing the word WATER. He doesn't understand that his gestures have any connection to something he needs or desires. It will be your task to repeatedly pair the gesture with the spoken word. Then provide him the much desired object or experience the signed word symbolizes when he performs the gesture you are showing him.

STEP THREE:
BABY EXPRESSES HIMSELF USING SIGNS

And now, parents everywhere, with no further ado: here is the event you have been waiting for! Your child is imitating your gestures and clearly understands the words you say and sign. Be on the lookout for his first bona fide signed word. You may not recognize it at first. Much like the eagerly awaited first movement of your child in the womb when you couldn't be certain if that internal "butterfly kiss" you felt was your baby or what you had for lunch, a baby's first sign is often easy to miss. He may perform the sign very differently than the way you modeled it for him.

So how do you know if your child is signing? Here are some hints:

○ *Your child repeats the same gesture.* "My daughter made the same motion whenever she heard music. That's how we figured out she was signing MUSIC. Once we understood what she was requesting, she was able to use her sign to tell us she wanted to hear music."

○ *The gesture appears to have a purpose and passion. He means business!* "I was talking to a friend at the grocery store and my daughter began to wave her hands. I continued to talk and she waved her hands again, but more vigorously this time. I resumed my conversation with my friend, and my daughter began flapping her arms again as if she were a bird preparing to take flight. It suddenly dawned on me that she was telling me she was ALL-DONE waiting for me to finish my visit with my friend."

○ *Each time he signs the word he may repeat a vocal sound. Often it is the initial consonant of the word.* "The first sign my son did was MORE. I asked him if he wanted more food as I signed MORE. He signed MORE back to me and said 'mo' with a lot of emphasis."

○ *Your child's proximity to a desired object gives you a clue.* For instance, the box of crackers is on the counter and he is tapping his arm. This may be his sign for CRACKER. "My daughter was watching me as I took the cheese out of the refrigerator. I turned around to hand her the cheese, and she began brushing her hands together. Instead of a twisting of the hands, it was more like when you wipe sand off of your hands. It was her version of CHEESE. I was so proud of her!"

○ *Your child's physical or mental state provides the context you need to determine what your child would likely be requesting.* Perhaps your child is very tired and begins to repeatedly perform the sign for BLANKET by pulling the gathered fingertips of both hands up toward his chin. "My son has a stuffed sheep his brother named Snuffy. We couldn't find him anywhere and it was nearing bedtime. My son was laying on our living room floor brushing his fingertips up his arm; I knew he was distraught that Snuffy was missing. This made it easier for me to figure out he was signing SHEEP."

○ *The situation provides the tip-off.* When your child pats his leg every time the DOG walks in the room or touches his forehead when he hears DADDY'S car drive into the garage, your attention is directed to your child's reaction to a change in his environment. "My daughter began to open and close her hands—her sign for BUBBLE—to request that I bring a bottle of bubbles when I told her we were going outside to play."

After your child has used one sign to communicate with you, he will likely learn several more fairly quickly. He loves how happy you are that he asked for something using his hands. He also likes getting what he wants at the wave of a hand—or the squeeze, tap, pat, or wiggle of a hand—whatever the sign requires!

Now that your child is imitating signs and using them to get what he wants, try asking for something with your words only. "I would sign ALL-DONE and then I would ask my daughter to sign ALL-DONE. After she consistently imitated my sign, I started saying and signing ALL-DONE, and then waiting for ten to fifteen seconds and then saying: "We are 'all done' now." I would ask her: "What are we?" and wait for her to show me her ALL-DONE sign."This technique will help your child learn to ask for what he wants or needs without having to see you sign the word for him. He needs to be able to recall the gestures all on his own to ask for what he needs without your prompt.

After young children can imitate gestures and understand that there is a connection between hand shapes and words, their sign vocabulary typically takes off. I have known children who waited six months before using their first signed word, and one week later they added twenty more signs to their conversations with others.

Continue to take your child's lead in adding new signs. Focus on what interests him and what he most often requests. After he expresses himself using single words for awhile, try combining signs into two-word phrases.

Isaac shows Maizie how to sign BALL.

Your task isn't to sign—or sing—every word of a phrase. Simply sign the key word in a sentence as you speak to your child. When he begins to speak, he will likely drop the signs for the words he can say clearly enough to be understood. He may still resort to signing words when he is very excited, wants to emphasize his point, or feels he is simply too tired to talk.

If you haven't already used it—and even if you have—the *Baby Sing & Sign* book (see the "References and Resources" section, page 271) would be a helpful resource for you as you begin the process of teaching your child to sign words with music, play, and picture books. It contains instructions for teaching many practical and helpful signs, and the companion music CD is great for children of all ages.

SECRETS OF SIGNING SUCCESS

○ Make your sign teaching a natural part of your day. Language learning requires a meaningful context.

○ Take "baby steps" in incorporating the ideas from this book into your child's life. Play with a sign and a song for as long as it takes for both of you to feel confident that you have mastered the material.

○ You will undoubtedly tire of the songs and activities long before your child. But the goal of *Mealtime and Bedtime Sing & Sign* is to support your child's emerging speech—as well as his interest in playful exploration, books, and love of learning. This requires opportunities to practice. Remember: *Repetition is good. Repetition is good. Repetition is good.*

○ Remind yourself often that the real reason for introducing sign language and singing is to enjoy and bond with your baby!

HAND FORMATIONS

The adult models in pictures throughout the book demonstrate the vocabulary using American Sign Language. Here are some key hand formations that you will use to perform basic sign vocabulary. When referred to in the book, hand formations appear in italics.

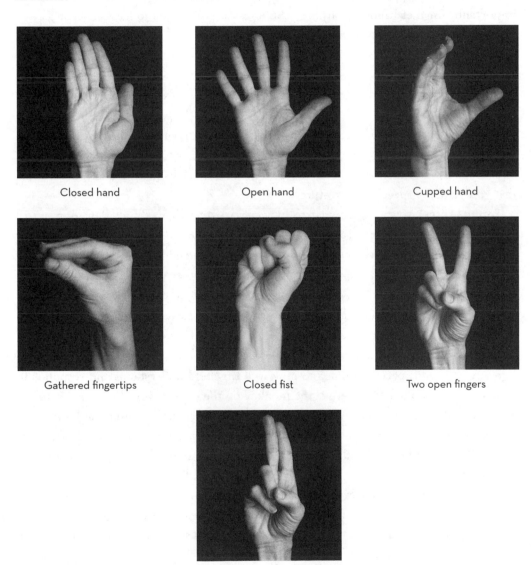

Closed hand

Open hand

Cupped hand

Gathered fingertips

Closed fist

Two open fingers

Two closed fingers

Note that teaching finger spelling and extensive ASL vocabulary is beyond the scope of this book. If you are interested in learning ASL in more depth, courses may be available in your community that teach the grammar, syntax, and vocabulary unique to American Sign Language, which is utilized in communication with most deaf adults. In addition, several online sign language dictionaries provide short video clips of thousands of signs (see the "References and Resources" section, page 271). Many parents find these to be helpful in learning new signs to teach their child that have meaning and importance for their whole family.

SPEECH DEVELOPMENT

The goal of teaching babies and toddlers sign language is to support the development of their emerging speech. You are giving them the opportunity to "flex their language muscles" as their vocal mechanism and language processing skills develop, so it is essential that you combine speech with gesture.

Parents often worry about what to expect regarding their child's development of speech. *When should my child be talking? How many words should he be saying and how often?* This is particularly true when their first- or second-born child provides a point of comparison for their baby's language skills. Perhaps big brother or sister talked sooner or more often than the new baby. Most experts agree that, in general, firstborn and girl babies are the earliest to talk, and there is a wide range of what is considered to be normal language development in children.

Parents should pay attention not only to what infants and toddlers express through sign language and speech, but also to how well the child understands and responds to what others say to him. ("Where is the monkey on the page of your book? Point to the monkey in the picture.") The American Academy of Pediatrics suggests that by twenty-four months, toddlers should be able to combine two or three spoken words into sentences. They should also be able to follow simple instructions and repeat words they hear in conversation.

This book will help you create activities that you can enjoy with your child while connecting with him in a meaningful way. Although research does suggest that the use of signing can enhance children's overall communication skills, this may not be the case for every child. The activities and information in this book are in no way intended to substitute for the expertise and assistance of a speech-language pathologist and are not meant to replace speech or language therapy. If you have any concerns about the development of your child, particularly in the area of communication, please talk to your pediatrician or contact your local school district for screening information.

Maizie signs MUSIC.

MEALTIME AND BEDTIME DICTIONARY

MEALTIME AND BEDTIME SIGNS

NOTE: Key mealtime vocabulary words are marked with ☀ *and important bedtime words are marked with* ☽ *. This can guide you in choosing a core vocabulary list if you are just beginning to teach your baby or toddler to sign.*

AGAIN

see Mealtime Bonus Signs (page 164)

ALL-DONE ☀

Hold *open hands* in front of you with palms toward chest. Flip hands to palms facing down.

Child may throw hands up to shoulders or shake hands from side to side.

♪ Tips for teaching the sign for ALL-DONE

○ Use at the conclusion of mealtime so your child can show you he is finished eating: "Are you ALL-DONE with dinner?" This is a far more attractive alternative than whining, fussing, or tossing his plate off his high chair tray.

○ ALL-DONE can be incorporated throughout your daily life with your child: ALL-DONE with your child's bedtime rituals, car ride, doctor's appointment, playtime, temper tantrum, your phone conversation or snack preparations.

○ The ALL-DONE sign gives your child a sense of control over his destiny. Once he sees you sign ALL-DONE or acknowledge his ALL-DONE sign, he is then able to predict with some certainty what will happen next. For example, when your child is ALL-DONE with his snack, he gets to get down from his high chair.

♪ Songs to sing and sign ALL-DONE

4. Fill the Basket (page 192)
7. Mister Moon (page 204)
11. Rainbows, Railroads, and Rhymes (page 220)

ALL-GONE

see Mealtime Bonus Signs (page 164)

ALRIGHT

see FINE (page 76)

APPLE and APPLESAUCE

Twist knuckle of
pointer finger on cheek.

Child may touch or
place palm on cheek.

Applesauce
(APPLE + SPOON)
Place curved pointer finger
at cheek and twist forward.
Then, *two closed fingers* scoop
across other *cupped*
hand (palm up) and up to
mouth as if eating from a bowl.
(SPOON is on page 168)

♪ Tips for teaching the sign for APPLE

○ Feed your child a spoonful of applesauce, and sign APPLE or APPLESAUCE as you ask her: "Do you like APPLE?" She will associate the taste of this delicious fruit with your signed word.

○ Show your child the picture of an apple on the jar of applesauce or package of dried apples. This helps her comprehend what apples look and taste like, as well as what the APPLE sign looks like.

○ Read books to your child that have pictures of apples in a variety of colors. Ask her to point to the APPLE on each page.

♪ Songs to sing and sign APPLE and APPLESAUCE

1. My Kitchen Door (page 182)
4. Fill the Basket (page 192)
12. Now I Lay Me Down to Sleep (page 224)

♪ Play, Sign, and Learn: APPLE

Shopping Trips

Trips to the grocery store are wonderful opportunities to teach sign language vocabulary. Babies and toddlers are natural people watchers and love to participate as you select food for your family. Make sure these excursions occur on days when you are not rushed and can "stop and smell the apples" instead of hurrying home to make supper. It is also a good idea to feed your child a snack before you arrive at the store.

Here are just a few ideas to make grocery shopping an educational field trip:

- Show her all the different colors of APPLES. Let her hold and smell them. Ask her to pick her favorite to buy for DADDY (page 61).
- Show her how to look for the freshest fruit. "Look at the BAD (page 28) spot on this fruit. It would taste YUCKY (page 28). Let's find an APPLE without bruises or spots."
- Hold an apple in one hand and a BANANA (page 29) in the other hand. Ask your child to touch or take the banana. Let her hold the banana in her hands as you sign and say: "Good finding the BANANA!" HIDE (page 91) the fruit behind your back and play the game again, reversing the fruit in your hands. Play this game with different fruit and vegetable choices as you add new food signs to your sign vocabulary.
- As you add each item to your grocery cart, be sure to say and sign "ALL-DONE (page 23) choosing _____ (food item)" before you look for your next item.
- Give your child food choices whenever possible: "Do you want PEACHES (page 121) or PEARS (page 122)? BREAD (page 40) or MUFFIN (page 109)? BEANS (page 164) or PEAS (page 123)?" Even little children love to make decisions about what they will eat.

BABY

Rock arms as if
holding a baby.

Child may place arms on
tummy and rock body.

♪ Tips for teaching the sign for BABY

○ The BABY sign uses the child's whole hand and is fairly easy for him to perform. Play a game with your child by saying and signing: "Who is my little BABY?" or "Where is my BABY?" It is important to look for facial expressions or other clues that your child comprehends your words and signs. This must happen first before he will begin to sign himself.

○ You can use the word BABY as a form of endearment for your child or can perform the BABY sign to show your child other human or animal babies you may see during your daily activities or in the books you read together.

♪ Songs to sing and sign BABY

6. What Did You Have for Your Supper? (page 200)
9. White Sheep and Black Sheep (page 212)
10. What'll We Do with the Baby? (page 215)

BAD/YUCKY

Put fingertips of *closed hand* to lips. Hand then moves down, as if tasting something bad and throwing it down.

Child may tap lips with fingertips and make a yucky face. Child may throw hands down once or several times.

♪ Tips for teaching the sign for BAD/YUCKY

○ The word BAD can be used by your child to express what she does not like. For example, when she lets you know through her body language and facial expression that she is frightened by loud noises, say: "That loud noise is BAD; I can tell it is scaring you!"

○ The sign for BAD can be used to help your child understand the things you want her to do for her own safety. For instance, you might tell your crawling baby: "BAD to touch oven, it is HOT (page 166)!"

○ Although I don't recommend teaching your child that a certain food is BAD, she may use the sign to let you know what she likes and doesn't like. You can acknowledge this by saying: "You are telling me you think CARROTS (page 49) are BAD but try just a bite. You may like them."

○ Never tell your child she is BAD. Rather, refer to her actions as BAD, and then redirect her with the preferred behavior. For the dog-feeding toddler, you might sign and say: "BAD to GIVE (page 84) Scruffy your FOOD (page 73), Scruffy needs DOG (page 67) FOOD. You eat your FOOD so you can grow big, big, big!"

○ Refer to teaching tips given for GOOD or YUMMY (page 86) for more ideas.

♪ Song to sing and sign BAD or YUCKY

5. John the Rabbit (page 195)

BAGEL

see Mealtime Bonus Signs (page 164)

BANANA

"Peel" pointer finger with *gathered fingertips* of other hand.

Child may brush fingertips with fingertips of other hand, or may simply point one finger.

♪ Tips for teaching the sign for BANANA

○ Sign food choices for your child, such as: "Do you want APPLE (page 25) or BANANA for your snack today?," so that he will want to receive that fruit in exchange for showing you the sign.

○ Show your child how you peel the banana before cutting it into bite-size pieces for him to eat. Let him help you peel the banana. Show him the sign for BANANA before and after you peel the fruit.

○ Picking up banana slices is good practice for your child's motor skills, as he figures out how to reach, grab, and hold the pieces and get them all the way into his mouth. Celebrate your child's ability to feed himself: "Way to go, little boy! You are eating the BANANA all by yourself!"

♪ Songs to sing and sign BANANA

4. Fill the Basket (page 192)
5. John the Rabbit (page 195)

SIGN SOLUTIONS: FLYING FOOD

Q: *Now that my son is eating finger foods, there seems to be more food on the floor than in his tummy. He also occasionally throws his food or dinnerware on the floor. Can sign language help me with our messy meals?*

Many skills practiced or modeled at mealtimes are just as important for health and growth as the food consumed. Mealtime for older babies is a time to refine the small motor movements he needs to grasp food off his plate with his fingers and operate a spoon. Most babies do not develop the ability to correctly use a spoon until twelve to fourteen months, but they should be given one to practice with well before that age. This will create messes. Some of the mess he is creating on your floor—and probably on his face and clothing—is necessary for him to learn how to feed himself. You may want to feed your baby in only his diaper during this time. Show him the sign for SPOON (page 168) to model the motion of eating with a utensil.

Some of his mealtime messiness may also be communication behavior. Perhaps he is choosing to communicate his mealtime wishes to you by throwing food or utensils on the floor to "say" that he is ALL-DONE with eating. The sign for ALL-DONE (page 23) is a powerful tool for teaching your child how to tell you he is finished eating and wants to get down from the high chair or table. When you notice he has stopped eating, sign and say: "Are you ALL-DONE or do you want MORE (page 107)?" If he throws his food or dinnerware, say and sign STOP (page 149) and prompt him by using your hands on his to perform the ALL-DONE sign. Then praise him for "using his words" to tell you what he wanted. Improving communication with your baby through signing can help with any behavioral concerns you have, including feeding challenges.

BARNYARD

see Lullaby Bonus Signs (page 173)

BASEBALL

see Lullaby Bonus Signs (page 173)

BATH OR WASH

Closed *fists* with thumbs on sides of fists scrub up and down on chest as if taking a bath.

Child may rub *open hands* or fists on chest or arm.

♪ Tips for teaching the sign for BATH/WASH

- ○ Make bathtime a special one for you and your child to share as you talk, sign, laugh, and play. Model the sign for BATH in advance of tub time: "After dinner, I will give you a nice, warm BATH." This will help him anticipate when bathtime occurs in his daily routine.
- ○ Add some nested plastic measuring cups so your child can practice pouring and filling them with water. Your child can also wash small plastic toy animals as you show him the signs for each. A few animals included in this book are DUCK (page 71), CAT (page 51), DOG (page 67), and PIG (page 124).

♪ Songs to sing and sign BATH/WASH

8. We're Having a Bath (page 208)
10. What'll We Do with the Baby? (page 215)

BATHROOM

see Bedtime Bonus Signs (page 170)

BEANS

see Mealtime Bonus Signs (page 164)

BEAR

Cross hands on body and scratch, showing a "bear hug."

Child may scratch shoulders or tummy without crossing her arms.

♪ Tips for teaching the sign for BEAR

○ Use the BEAR sign to label the wide variety of bears in your child's world, from the cuddly stuffed bear he snuggles each night in bed to the real bears you and your child can visit at the local zoo.

○ Include your BEAR sign as part of your nighttime rituals if a stuffed bear is your child's comfort object. If your child's favorite snuggle partner is a stuffed duck, give that much-loved item its own sign name: DUCK (page 71). Signing each component of your nighttime ritual, such as BATH (page 31), BOOK (page 38), and KISS (page 94), will provide comfort as he prepares himself for bed.

○ Play a game of pretend by telling your child with your hands and your voice that he is the BABY (page 27) BEAR and you are the MOMMY (page 104) or DADDY (page 61) BEAR. With your little bear on your lap, sign BEAR with your arms in front of his chest.

♪ Song to sing and sign BEAR

8. We're Having a Bath (page 208)

♪ Play, Sign, and Learn: BEAR

Honey Bear Shaker

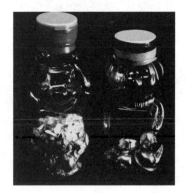

Materials:
- Empty, clean bear-shaped honey container
- Colorful buttons, rice, popcorn, or beans
- Superglue or hot-glue gun and glue stick

As toddlers, children begin to understand that objects can represent words such as BEAR. This is a first step for your child toward playing games using his imagination. To make a fun Bear Shaker, thoroughly wash an empty bear-shaped honey container. Fill halfway with colorful buttons, rice, popcorn, or beans. Using a hot-glue gun or Superglue, glue both the screw-top and the flip-top so that they cannot be unfastened by even the most persistent toddler fingers.

Tell your son: "I can make MUSIC (page 111) with my BEAR." Sing "la, la, la" or a simple musical story about your bear using any notes you choose! ("My BEAR LOVES (page 98) my little BOY (page 39), and I LOVE him, too . . .")

All homemade toys require adult supervision and need to be routinely checked to be sure they are safe. The contents of the Bear Shaker could pose a choking hazard if swallowed.

BEAUTIFUL

see Bedtime Bonus Signs (page 170)

BED/SLEEP and TIRED

Place head on *closed hand* palm side up as if head rests on pillow (BED/SLEEP).

Place fingertips of *cupped hands* on chest; then roll hands forward and slump shoulders as if fatigued (TIRED).

Bed

Child may place one or both hands on head and tap several times. Child will likely use BED/SLEEP sign for TIRED as well, as their meanings are interchangeable to a young child.

♪ Tips for teaching the sign for BED/SLEEP/TIRED

○ Use the BED sign as a cue for two of the more predictable events in your child's life: naptime in the morning—or afternoon or both—and bedtime at the end of the day. Most children are reluctant to admit that they are ready to sleep, so try telling her that you or one of her stuffed animals is tired. Then lay your head or the toy on your child's pillow.

○ You can make a picture book of your child's bedtime routine, and call it "_____'s *[insert your child's name] Bedtime.*" Have someone photograph you and your child doing each step in the bedtime routine. Paste them in order into the blank pages of a small binder or photo album. Your daughter can then "read" you her special book and point to the pictures as you ask her to.

○ Try some imaginative play with your child. Close your eyes and sign BED. Tell her you are sleeping. Ask her to wake you up with a HUG (page 98) or a KISS (page 94). When you feel her touch you, open your eyes and tell her, "Thank you for waking me up!" Ask her if she would like to take a turn playing the "Sleep and Wake" game.

○ Refer to teaching tips given for NIGHT-NIGHT (page 114) or "Sign Solutions" (page 99, 115) for more information and ideas about BED and SLEEP.

♪ Songs to sing and sign BED/SLEEP/TIRED

SIGN OF SUCCESS

"We taught our son the sign for SLEEP by always pointing out when a person or animal was sleeping: our family dog, a baby in a stroller on a walk, or a character in a book. This sign really helped in explaining our schedule for the day or anticipating when something was going to happen. ('DADDY (page 61) will be home after your NAP.')"

—Chrissy S.

BIB

see Mealtime Bonus Signs (page 164)

BIG

see Mealtime Bonus Signs (page 164)

BIRD

Thumb and pointer finger
of one hand open and
close at mouth in imitation
of bird's mouth.

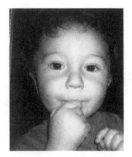

Child may touch mouth
with pointer finger, or
open and close hand to
imitate bird's beak.

♪ Tips for teaching the sign for BIRD

○ Put your child in his stroller and take a walk. Point out birds you and your child see flying, walking, hopping, singing, and resting. Say and sign BIRD each time you see a bird in action.

○ Children love sound play. From infancy, they begin the slow process of coordinating their lips, tongue, teeth, and breath to imitate the sounds they hear. "What sound does the BIRD make?" Sign BIRD as you make the sound: "peep, peep" or "tweet, tweet." Tell your child it is his turn to make the BIRD sound.

♪ Songs to sing and sign BIRD

1. My Kitchen Door (page 182)
9. White Sheep and Black Sheep (page 212)

BLANKET

Open hands in front of chest pull to *closed fists* as if pulling blanket up to chin.

Child may bring fists up to chin.

♪ Tips for teaching the sign for BLANKET

○ The sign for BLANKET may be an important one for your child if this is her security object. Luckily, this sign is easy for children to perform as it uses whole hand shapes.

○ Cover your child's head with a lightweight blanket and ask her, "WHERE (page 162) is my little GIRL (page 83)?" Then dramatically pull the blanket off your child as you say: "Peek-a-boo, I see you!" If your child prefers to be able to see you as you play the game, simply drape the blanket across the top of her head so that she can watch your hands and see your face.

○ Make a "Baby Blanket Burrito": Have your toddler lie on the edge of a child-sized blanket with her arms at her sides, and then gently roll her and the blanket, being careful not to cover her face, until she is wrapped burrito-style. You can use this as a variation of "Peek-a-boo" and ask: "Where is my little GIRL?" when she is wrapped in the blanket. Then gently unroll her and exclaim: "There she is!" You can also make up your own words for the game, signing "BLANKET BABY, come out, come out!" or another phrase of your own creation. This game is also wonderful sensory stimulation for your child. The cloth on her skin and gentle rolling promotes her sense of touch, balance, and coordination.

♪ Song to sing and sign BLANKET

10. What'll We Do with the Baby? (page 215)
11. Rainbows, Railroads, and Rhymes (page 220)

BOAT

see Bedtime Bonus Signs (page 170)

BOOK

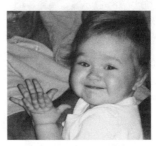

Place *closed hands* together and then open them as if opening a book.

Child may either place palms open or closed, but not do opening motion.

♪ Tips for teaching the sign for BOOK

○ Use the sign for BOOK as an activity choice: "Would you like to PLAY (page 126) or read a BOOK?" Babies and toddlers love you to read aloud to them. Nestled in your lap, the sound of your voice is soothing and music to your child's ears.

○ Use your signs to show your child his schedule of activities. "Now we will EAT (page 73) breakfast; then we will BRUSH-TEETH (page 42), read BOOKS (page 38), and go to the STORE (page 150) for groceries." Or "First let's PLAY with toys, and then we'll read a BOOK."

○ Use a sign to describe some of your child's favorite books. Ask him to find his DOG (page 67) BOOK or his SHOE (page 138) BOOK. Ask him to sign his preference for the books he would like to read at bedtime.

♪ Song to sing and sign BOOK

11. Rainbows, Railroads, and Rhymes (page 220)

BOWL

see Mealtime Bonus Signs (page 164)

BOY

Place *fingers* of one hand at forehead as if holding the bill of a baseball cap.

Child may tap fingers or *open hand* on forehead, brow, or cheek.

♪ Tips for teaching the sign for BOY

○ Learning to figure out whether someone is a BOY or a GIRL (page 83) often takes years for a young child to master. Give children the chance to interact with BOYS and GIRLS and figure out the observable differences between friends of both genders. They may also forget whether they themselves are a BOY or a GIRL. It is good to remind them by saying and signing phrases like: "You are such a GOOD (page 86) BOY" or "are you DADDY'S (page 61) BOY?"

○ Young children love to look at photographs of other babies and toddlers. As you read books together, ask your child to touch the picture of the BOY or GIRL on the page.

○ Refer to teaching tips given for GIRL for more ideas.

♪ Song to sing and sign BOY

2. Crawly, Creepy Little Mousie (page 185)

BREAD

Fingertips of *cupped hand* repeatedly brush across top of other *cupped hand,* showing slices in loaf of bread.

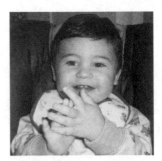

Child may tap top of hand with fingertips.

♪ Tips for teaching the sign for BREAD

○ When your child is able to pick up bits of food and put them in his mouth, he is ready for bread. Start with tiny bits of the soft inner slice of toast. They will soften in his mouth so he can swallow them. As you introduce this new food to him, sign BREAD before and after you give him a bread bite.

○ Finger foods are equal parts nutrition and play materials for babies. Many of the bread cubes you set on your child's high chair tray will end up on the floor. Praise your child for every bite of bread that makes it to his mouth: "WHERE (page 162) is your BREAD? Good job EATING (page 73) your BREAD!"

○ You can use the BREAD sign for bites of biscuit, rice cake, or loaves such as applesauce or carrot bread. You want your child to learn that BREAD comes in a variety of colors, textures, shapes, and tastes.

♪ Songs to sing and sign BREAD

1. My Kitchen Door (page 182)
3. The Muffin Man (page 188)

♪ Play, Sign, and Learn: BREAD

Babies and Bread

By eight months, bread can usually be introduced to babies as a new texture and another finger-food option. It is best to select whole-grain bread without added sugar or salt from the start. The bread should also have a texture that dissolves readily in your child's mouth. In *What to Expect the First Year* (Workman Publishing), the authors suggest BAGELS (page 164) that have been frozen as a great first experience with bread. They are harder than bread, and your baby can scrape off the exterior and "chew" this mushy substance with his gums. Rice cakes are another bread option, as the pieces the baby breaks off will dissolve in his mouth.

Some children have allergic reactions to eggs or glutens (found in bread made from wheat, oats, rye, or barley). The risk for skin rashes and other allergic reactions diminishes after the first year. To be safe, always add only one new type of food at a time, including varieties of breads and other baked goods.

Eating bread can pose a choking hazard to young children. To keep your child from choking on bread:

- *Avoid white bread, which can turn pasty with saliva.*
- *Remove crusts and cube the bread before giving it to your child.*
- *Make sure your baby is seated in an upright position when eating.*
- *No bread, cracker, or teething biscuit—commercially prepared or homemade—is guaranteed to not break off or crumble. Always supervise your child carefully when he is eating.*

Rachel Paxton, mother of four and author of *What's for Dinner?* (www.creative homemaking.com), provides this recipe for homemade bread sticks. She recommends them as a teething biscuit for older children.

Banana Bread Teething Biscuits

¹/2 cup shortening
1 cup sugar
2 eggs
3 bananas, mashed
2 cups flour
¹/2 cup wheat germ
1 teaspoon baking soda
¹/4 teaspoon salt

- Preheat oven to 350 degrees.
- Cream shortening, sugar, and eggs, then add mashed bananas and mix well.
- Blend in the other ingredients.
- Pour into a greased loaf pan. Bake for about 45 minutes. Once the bread has cooled, slice it into sticks and bake at 150–200 degrees for 1 hour. Store in an airtight container.

(Copyright © 2007 by Rachel Paxton. Reprinted with permission.)

BREAKFAST

see EAT (page 73)

BROTHER

see Lullaby Bonus Signs (page 173)

BRUSH-TEETH

Pointer finger moves
back and forth in front
of teeth in imitation
of a toothbrush.

Child may touch teeth
with pointer finger.

♪ Tips for teaching the sign for BRUSH-TEETH

○ Dentists agree that tooth brushing should begin as soon as a baby's first tooth appears (usually around four to seven months), and that by age two, your child should have her teeth brushed at least once a day, preferably at bedtime.

○ The sign for BRUSH-TEETH shows your child what it looks like to brush as your finger imitates the motion you use inside your mouth to clean your teeth. You will need to brush your child's teeth for her until she has the fine motor skills to brush on her own.

○ Use your BRUSH-TEETH sign to establish teeth brushing as part of your mealtime or bedtime routines. Play a tooth brushing game of "Find the Hidden Teeth." Say and sign: "It is time to BRUSH your TEETH. Where are your teeth HIDING (page 91)? Is there one over here? Over here? Oh, there's a tooth!"

♪ Song to sing and sign BRUSH-TEETH

8. We're Having a Bath (page 208)

BUBBLE

Using both hands, open and close *gathered fingertips* as you move them in the air like bubbles floating up in the sky.

Child may open and close fingertips without additional movement.

♪ Tips for teaching the sign for BUBBLE

○ Blow bubbles so that your child can see them at eye level. Say and sign the word BUB-BLE, and then sign the word again as you ask him: "Do you like BUBBLES?" Help him sign it by taking his hands in yours. Then tell him: "Good job telling me BUBBLES! Here are some MORE (page 107)."

○ Toddlers love to practice counting, and can often count up to three objects. Sign the word BUBBLE as you say: "One BUBBLE, two BUBBLES, three BUBBLES!" You can point to the bubble in the air as you say "one," "two," and "three."

Song to sing and sign BUBBLE

8. We're Having a Bath (page 208)

SIGN OF SUCCESS

"I use bubbles to calm my son when he becomes agitated. There is something hypnotic for him about the slow, quiet movement of the 'little balls' in the air. We also use bubbles to entertain ourselves when we must wait for someone or something: for daddy to come home, for muffins to finish baking in the oven, for our cat to wake up from her snooze so we can play with her. As the bubbles float, we sign BUBBLE and say 'bubble' or 'pop'!"

—Carri K.

Play, Sign, and Learn: BUBBLE

Bubble Magic

> "Tiny bubbles . . . make me happy, make me feel fine."
> —Don Ho (1966)

Children are fascinated by bubbles and many a toddler has been consoled by these mysterious circles of air. Whether homemade or purchased from a store, bubbles can provide hours of enjoyment.

Research has determined that bubble time can also be beneficial to children. According to a new study funded by the Economic and Social Research Council (ESRC), "youngsters who can lick their lips, blow bubbles, and pretend that a building block is a car are most likely to find learning language easy." Dr. Katie Alcock at Lancaster University has also discovered strong links between language abilities and mouth movements and fine motor skills (see "References and Resources," page 271). As parents, we now have even more motivation to include bubble time in our play agendas.

Bubble play is very popular and bubble toys are now available with numerous accessories and come in a variety of shapes, colors, and sizes. Here are some suggestions for bubble magic with your toddler:

- Look for spill-proof containers to ease the mess and clean-up process.
- Search for wands with large openings to "catch" the bubble solution.
- To ease your toddler's frustrations as he struggles to blow the bubbles, use a drinking straw cut to approximately three inches and hold it up to the bubble wand to assist your toddler in directing his breath. Show him how to put the drinking straw between his lips and blow. Then hold it in position and give him a turn.
- Although many battery-operated bubble blowers are available, do not let them be a substitute for "true" bubble blowing.
- Add a drop or two of washable paint to your bubble solution. Hang a piece of paper on an easel or outdoor fence and blow your bubbles in the direction of the paper. Enjoy the design the bubbles create as they pop.
- Play music as you blow bubbles and encourage your child to dance through the bubbles. Vary the style and tempo of music and encourage your child to modify his dancing to match the beat of the music.
- Give him a butterfly net, a small scoop, or a bowl to use to capture his bubbles.

Bubble solutions require adult supervision and need to be monitored closely.

BUG

Place thumb on nose with pointer and middle finger extended. Bend the pointer and middle fingers several times as if they are bug antennae.

Child may place fist on nose or thumb of *open hand* while bending all fingers.

♪ Tips for teaching the sign for BUG

○ For most babies and toddlers, bugs are any small insect, including spiders, flies, beetles, bees, ants, roly-polies, caterpillars, and ladybugs. If your child is fearful of bugs, give these pesky creatures a signed name to help alleviate her fear: "There is a BUG on your stroller. Mommy will shoo it away. Goodbye, BUG!"

○ Babies and toddlers love to move and sound like animals—and bugs, too! Show your child how to crawl like a BUG. Make the "bzzzzz" sound of a flying insect and see if your child will imitate your voice. Let her watch your face. Is she trying to make her lips and tongue form the same shape as yours? Sign BUG as you "bzzzzz."

♪ Song to sing and sign BUG

2. Crawly, Creepy Little Mousie (page 185)

♪ Play, Sign, and Learn: BUG

Jar of Ladybugs

Materials:
- Three small, flat stones, washed and dried, and large enough so that they cannot fit through a toilet paper roll
- Child-safe red tempera paint (optional: other paint colors to make various bugs)
- Child-sized chunky paintbrush or sponge brush
- "Sloppy shirt" for child to wear while painting
- Black permanent marker (for parent's use only)
- Plastic peanut butter jar—clean and label removed

Put your child in an old shirt so you don't need to worry about her getting messy. Make a bug with your toddler. The candidate for friendliest bug is the ladybug. Find a small flat stone that your child can easily hold in her hand. ***To make sure it doesn't pose a choking hazard to your toddler, check that the stone cannot fit through a toilet paper roll.*** Using red paint and a paintbrush, show your child how to paint the stone. When the stone is dry, you can add the black stripe down your bug's back and add her black dots with marker (as shown).

Help your child unscrew the lid from the plastic peanut butter jar. Show her how to drop her bug into the jar. Make two or three ladybugs while you are painting your stones, so that your child will have several to add to the bug jar.

- Count your bugs as you drop them into the jar: "one BUG, two BUGS. . . ." Sign the word BUG each time you add a bug to the jar.
- Help your toddler screw the lid on top of the jar. Shake the jar and make bug music. Sing and sign the "Crawly, Creepy Little Mousie song (page 185), replacing "mousie" with "buggie" as your child accompanies your singing with her musical bug shaker.
- Paint a yellow lightning bug, a green grasshopper, or a black spider, using stones and your imagination. Add them to the bug jar.

BUTTERFLY

Cross wrists and link thumbs. Then bend fingers of both *open hands* several times like the flapping wings of a butterfly.

Child may bend fingers of both hands without crossing wrists or may place the back of one hand on the palm of the other and bend fingers.

♪ Tips for teaching the sign for BUTTERFLY

○ Butterflies are everywhere—stickers, small toys, clothing, home décor—and their shape and bright colors are easily recognizable to small children. Search for butterflies throughout your daily outings with your baby: "Oh look, sweetheart, a BUTTERFLY!"

○ Visit a nature center, nursery, or park and watch for butterflies. The BUTTERFLY sign is quite visual and matches the movements of the butterfly. It is an easy sign for baby to recognize and a motivating one for them to attempt themselves. The linked thumbs will be difficult for baby and toddler fingers. Your child may simply wiggle fingertips slightly, or watch his own hands to make sure that what his brain "told" his fingers to do is actually occurring! Smile and praise liberally: "Yes, I see you signing BUTTERFLY. Great job!"

♪ Song to sing and sign BUTTERFLY

9. White Sheep and Black Sheep (page 212)

CAKE

see Mealtime Bonus Signs (page 164)

CARROT

Place *closed fist* with thumb on fingers at side of mouth and pretend to eat carrot.

Child may touch mouth with fingers or place fist on cheek without pretending to eat.

♪ Tips for teaching the sign for CARROT

○ Use the signed and spoken word CARROT before you present this food to your child: "Would you like some CARROT for lunch?" Repeat the spoken word CARROT as you feed your baby. Say and sign CARROT as you watch your hungry toddler eat her cooked carrot slices.

○ Play "Hide the Carrots." Hold a bowl of carrots behind your back or cover them with an opaque plastic container. Sign and say: "WHERE (page 162) are the CARROTS? The CARROTS are HIDING (page 91). Can you find them?" Ask her to "tell you" CARROT with her hands and then take the carrots from their hiding place. Show your toddler how to cover the carrots and hide them from you. It is your turn to sign CARROT to get the carrots back!

♪ Songs to sing and sign CARROT

4. Fill the Basket (page 192)
5. John the Rabbit (page 195)
6. What Did You Have for Your Supper? (page 200)

SIGN SOLUTIONS: PICKY EATERS

Q: *I want to provide the best nutrition possible for my daughter, but she is very particular about what she eats. Can sign language help me convince my child to try new foods and eat nutritiously?*

Toddlers are often picky about the foods they eat. Your daughter is asserting her budding independence in all areas of her life, including what she chooses to eat. Some children are also sensitive to certain tastes and textures of foods. Unlike adults, who often acquire tastes for exotic or peculiar food such as oysters and sushi, children are not adventurous by nature when it comes to tasting.

It is important that you do not become angry or anxious in response to mealtime issues. Bribes and forcing food should also be avoided. Offer only one new food per mealtime. Your baby may not touch it the first few times she sees it; she is getting used to having it on her plate. Continue to provide a wide variety of foods to taste and try, including many fresh fruits and vegetables. And "if at first you don't succeed, try, try again!" She may not try green BEANS (page 164) the first time they appear on her plate, but she will probably try them if they show up on her plate a dozen more times. If you are providing nutritious choices for her and she continues to grow and gain weight, you should not be overly concerned with what she eats.

You can model healthy eating habits for your child by signing as you eat the foods you offer to her. Show her with your animated facial expression and signed words that you think the foods are YUMMY (page 86), including FRUIT (page 80), MEAT (page 101), CARROTS (page 49), and CORN (page 58), to name a few.

Prepare only one meal for your child; you don't want to become a short-order cook! If she refuses to eat what is offered, sign ALL-DONE and redirect her to another activity. Do not try and force her. Her nutrition needs are met by what she eats throughout the day, and not as a result of eating three substantial meals.

You can incorporate the colors of the rainbow on your child's plate. Sign RAINBOW (page 174) and point out the different colors of foods she will eat as she finishes her meal. Ask her, "Did you EAT a RAINBOW" for lunch?" (See page 117 for more great food suggestions in the "Fruit and Vegetable Rainbow.")

Snack time is your child's chance to choose foods she likes to eat, such as BANANA (page 29), PEAR (page 122), CRACKER (page 60), or bites of BAGEL (page 164). Encourage her to tell you "with her hands" what she wants to eat. Giving her choices at snack time may lessen the likelihood that you will have food power struggles at mealtimes.

CAT

Pull pinched thumb and pointer finger from cheek to show cat's whiskers.

Child may brush cheek with pointer finger or fingertips.

♪ Tips for teaching the sign for CAT

○ Show your child the CAT sign and ask him: "What sound does the CAT make?" or "What does the CAT say?" When you make the "meow" sound for your child, sign CAT at the same time. With practice, your child will likely sign CAT as he "meows."

○ As you touch toy cats, pictures of cats in books, or an extremely cooperative pet cat of your own, call your child's attention to the body parts of the kitty: "Where are the CAT's ears? CAT's feet? CAT's tummy? CAT's nose? CAT's mouth?" This is an opportunity for your child to compare and contrast things that are the same and different in animals and people. Does your child have a tail? (No.) Does your child have fur? (No.) Does your child say "meow" when you pet him? (Probably!)

♪ Song to sing and sign CAT

1. My Kitchen Door (page 182)

CEREAL

Scoop one *cupped hand* across the other and up to mouth as if eating cereal from a bowl.

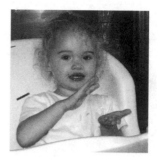

Child may lift both *cupped hands* to mouth.

♪ Tips for teaching the sign for CEREAL

○ This sign for cereal represents cereal eaten with a spoon, either baby cereal or boxed cereal eaten with milk. Boxed cereal Os that baby eats with her fingers can be signed by forming an O shape with the thumb touching *gathered fingertips.*

○ Mealtime is playtime for older babies. Your child loves the independence of being able to feed herself morsels of food. Pieces of dry cereal help her practice her dexterity and ability to pass something from one hand to the other.

○ Play a "HIDE (page 91) the CEREAL" game. Give her some small pieces of cereal to hold with her fingers and dip into applesauce or yogurt. Hide a piece of cereal in applesauce or yogurt and let her feel for it with her fingers, and then gobble it up.

♪ Song to sing and sign CEREAL

1. My Kitchen Door (page 182)

♪ Play, Sign, and Learn: CEREAL

Cereal Sun Catchers

Materials:

- Fruit-flavored cereal Os or other colorful cereal
- One- or two-gallon sized freezer Ziploc bag
- Tablecloth or shower curtain
- Empty shaker bottle (a plastic spice bottle that has been thoroughly cleaned is the perfect size for little hands)
- Funnel
- Clear contact paper
- Scissors
- Yarn

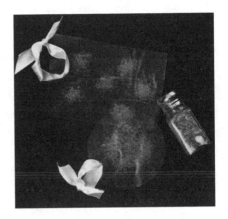

Children love to receive presents. They also experience great satisfaction in giving presents, especially presents they have made themselves. Cereal Sun Catchers are a great idea for a homemade art present for special people in your child's life.

Start by having your daughter put handfuls of fruit-flavored cereal Os into a Ziploc bag. Seal it for her, making sure you get all of the extra air out of the bag. Say and sign, "It's time to crush the CEREAL. You need to smash it with your SHOES (page 138)." Put a tablecloth or shower curtain on the floor and then place the Ziploc bag on top of it. Help your child smash the cereal by giving her your hand for support as she stomps. Make up a little chant as she works to crush the cereal, "Crush! Stomp! Smash! Crush! Stomp! Smash!" Show her what is happening to the cereal. Help her find the pieces that still need to be smashed. After your toddler begins to tire, use your shoes to finish up any remaining cereal pieces.

Next, put the funnel on your plastic shaker bottle, pour in your cereal "dust," and replace the shaker piece on the bottle. Cut contact paper into pairs of small circles, squares, and triangles (approximately 5 inches x 5 inches). Show the shapes to your child and say the name of each one for her. Move your tablecloth or shower curtain to a table or sit down on the floor to create your Cereal Sun Catchers. Have your child pick a shape and decide who will receive it as a present.

Now you are ready to create. Pull off the backing from the contact paper and lay it sticky side up. Let your little one use her new shaker full of cereal dust to create the sun catcher. Point out the colors that you see on the paper and tell her how much the recipient is going to love her present. Shake off the extra dust from her creation, peel off the backing from the matching contact paper shape, and cover her cereal dust. Make sure to pinch it tightly all along the edges. Let your little one hold it up to a window and admire how the bright sun shines on her art. Lastly, poke a small hole along one of the edges and tie a piece of yarn through the hole so that the recipient may display her new gift in a window.

- A fun variation is to sort the cereal pieces by color and crush them in individual Ziploc bags. Place the colors in their own shaker for other fun art creations.

Make only one or several and be sure to save your cereal dust for future projects.

All homemade toys require adult supervision and need to be routinely checked to be sure they are safe. The materials for Cereal Sun Catchers could pose a choking hazard if swallowed.

CHAIR OR SIT

Form two *closed fingers* with both hands. Place one on top of the other as if one hand "sits" on the other.

Child may place one hand on top of the other.

♪ Tips for teaching the sign for CHAIR/SIT

○ There are numerous variations on CHAIR and SIT for a baby and toddler: high chair, car seat, rocking chair, couch, child-sized chair, and "sit here right now!" When you are introducing the sign, try placing him on his bottom in the chair as you smile and say "sit," and then show him the sign immediately after.

○ Your family dog may be able to help you teach the word SIT. If your dog has mastered this command, ask him to SIT and then if he complies, say and sign: "Nice SIT, Scruffy!" Ask your child to say and sign SIT to Scruffy.

○ Play a simple game of musical chairs. Sing a song of your own choosing and sign MUSIC (page 111) as you stand near a chair. Next, stop singing and sit in the chair as you sign SIT. Repeat the game by singing and signing MUSIC as you walk to another chair. As you play, let your child point to all the furniture in your house that qualifies as a chair. Your child will probably think this is a hilariously funny game. We love tapping into baby's emerging sense of humor, as that means the child is enjoying the game while reaping the incidental educational benefits.

♪ Songs to sing and sign CHAIR/SIT

CHANGE

see Bedtime Bonus Signs (page 170)

CHEESE

Press palms of *open hands* together and twist, like pressing cheese.

Child may bring hands together or pat hands together several times.

♪ Tips for teaching the sign for CHEESE

○ Narrate a "cheese story" by saying and signing: "I love CHEESE. I EAT (page 73) CHEESE! CHEESE is YUMMY (page 86)," and any other statements you would like to make about cheese. Then offer your child some. Say and sign: "Do you want CHEESE? Show me." Take her hands and help her make the sign. Then tell her: "Good telling me you want CHEESE. Here you go." Give her a spoonful of cottage cheese or a small piece to hold and feed herself.

○ Give your child cheese choices: cottage or string? Yellow or white? Little or big piece? With or without CRACKER (page 60)? Several different textures and colors of edible substances are in the category of foods we call "cheese," and toddlers need to figure out what foods qualify.

♪ Songs to sing and sign CHEESE

1. My Kitchen Door (page 182)
2. Crawly, Creepy Little Mousie (page 185)
3. The Muffin Man (page 188)

CHOKE

see Mealtime Bonus Signs (page 164)

CLIMB

see Lullaby Bonus Signs (page 173)

COLD

see Mealtime Bonus Signs (page 164)

COMB-HAIR

Open fingers of
cupped hand comb hair.

Child may use fingers or
hand to comb hair or
touch or rub hair.

♪ Tips for teaching the sign COMB-HAIR

○ When your child can touch his hair without assistance, teach him the sign for COMB-HAIR. Sit in front of a mirror together and sign COMB-HAIR on the baby's head as if combing his hair. Use your fingers to "comb" your child's hair as well as your own.

○ The sign for COMB-HAIR pantomimes the action of pulling the teeth of a comb through your hair. Use an actual comb to show your child the sign. Comb your hair. Comb your child's hair. Comb a stuffed animal's "hair."

○ Sing and sign: "This is the way we COMB our HAIR" to the tune of "Here We Go 'Round the Mulberry Bush." Add verses about other hygiene rituals: BRUSH our TEETH (page 42), take a BATH (page 31), EAT our FOOD (page 73).

♪ Song to sing and sign COMB-HAIR

8. We're Having a Bath (page 208)

COOK

see Mealtime Bonus Signs (page 164)

COOKIE

see Mealtime Bonus Signs (page 164)

CORN

Grasp imaginary corn cob
with fingertips and rotate
it forward as you
pretend to eat it.

Child may put
both fists to mouth.

♪ Tips for teaching the sign for CORN

○ As she grows, allow your child to see and taste corn in its different forms: from creamed corn to steamed corn on the cob. Let your child HELP (page 90) you pull the husks off the ear of corn.

○ Animals love to eat corn. Visit a farm or petting zoo where you are allowed to FEED (page 73) the ROOSTER (page 134) or PIG (page 124) some CORN. Put dried corn on the cob on a stick and make a BIRD (page 36) feeder for the backyard. Watch the HUNGRY (page 93) animals as they eat corn.

♪ Song to sing and sign CORN

5. John the Rabbit (page 195)

♪ Play, Sign, and Learn: CORN

Corncob Designs

Materials:
- Large pieces of drawing paper
- Tablecloth or shower curtain
- Washable paint
- 1 or 2 baking pans

Keep art activities interesting by using new materials. Corn on the cob is a fun new material to use when painting. Children love touching the ridges and bumps of corn, and they love it even more when the corn is covered in colorful paint.

To make your corncob designs, first set out your tablecloth or shower curtain on the floor or a table and cover it with your drawing paper. Next, put washable paint in a baking pan or other flat container with sides. Then, cut the corn on the cob in half and roll the two pieces in the paint.

Tell your child, "It's time to paint with CORN. Let's get our hands in the paint and roll the CORN on the paper." Your child will giggle with delight as you model the painting process. Roll the paint-covered corncobs across the paper. Have fun while you paint. Make funny sounds as the corn rolls across the paper. Roll the corn in different directions, and even add a different color or two. Your child will love having messy fun with you.

- Try standing the corn on the cob on end in the paint and use the end to make corn stamp prints on your paper.
- Dress up your corncob designs by sprinkling glitter on the wet paint. Talk about how the corn designs sparkle.
- Try painting with other fruits and vegetables. Which ones are better for rolling? Which ones are better for stamping? Which ones are better for brushing? Compare the different fruit and vegetable creations to your corncob design. Also, try rolling grapes, plums, oranges, and grapefruit and compare the size of the lines they make.

Your child will never look at produce the same.

Supervise your child with the paint-covered fruit and vegetables. Your child may try to taste the food without giving consideration to the paint that is covering them.

CRACKER

Tap one *closed fist* on elbow of the other arm.

Child may touch hand or fingertips to other arm or hand.

♪ Tips for teaching the sign for CRACKER

○ Say and sign sentences about crackers such as: "Here is a CRACKER. I EAT (page 73) CRACKER. You EAT CRACKER." Then eat the cracker. Follow by saying and signing CRACKER again.

○ Snacks can be a time of play and exploration for your child. As he plays, he is practicing important skills for coordinating his hands, wrists, fingers, lips, and tongue that enable him to feed himself. Let him put crackers into all the cups of a muffin tin; show him how to put a cracker in each hole. Point to each container or compartment in the muffin tin and ask him: "What's that?" The repetition will likely amuse him and will be great practice for his new CRACKER sign. ***Be certain you are close by to supervise cracker play so that he does not put too many crackers in his mouth at one time.***

○ Have a picnic in your backyard with lots of finger foods, including crackers. Spread a cloth on the ground and set a place for your child's favorite stuffed animal. Let the child choose what the animal would like for his supper: CRACKER? BANANA (page 29)? PEAS (page 123)?

♪ Songs to sing and sign CRACKER

2. Crawly, Creepy Little Mousie (page 185)
3. The Muffin Man (page 188)

CUP

see Mealtime Bonus Signs (page 164)

CURTAIN

see Bedtime Bonus Signs (page 170)

DADDY

Place thumb of
open hand on forehead.

Child may place fingertips or
palm on forehead or head.

♪ Tips for teaching the sign for DADDY

○ Fathers can use this sign to refer to themselves, as they say and sign sentences such as: "DADDY loves to play with you, little boy!" or "DADDY needs you to EAT (page 73) your breakfast now."

○ Other people can also say and sign DADDY in his absence. If daddy is close by, you might say and sign: "Do you see DADDY?" or "WHERE (page 162) is DADDY?" If your child looks in the direction of the doorway or scans the room in search of his father, he has made the connection between the word and the person called "daddy." Strengthen this learning by saying and signing sentences such as: "I see you looking for DADDY. Let's go find him."

○ Refer to teaching tips given for MOMMY (page 104) for more ideas.

♪ Songs to sing and sign DADDY

DANCE

Swing *two open fingers*
over other upward-facing
palm as if dancing
back and forth.

Child may tap fingertips
on palm or simply
wiggle her body and arms.

♪ Tips for teaching the sign for DANCE

○ Put on your *Mealtime and Bedtime Sing & Sign* CD and show your child your fancy dance moves. Encourage him to move to the music by signing and saying: "Let's DANCE, DANCE, DANCE!" Isolate the body part motions of dancing by directing him to "DANCE with your arms," "DANCE with your feet," and so on.

○ Babies and toddlers love you to hold them while you dance. To calm your child, rhythmically swing him, rock him in a slow and sustained way, and keep his head level. For a livelier dance, change the speed or rhythm or your movements and the position of his head with some tips and twirls. Dancing in a variety of ways will help him learn that all of these experiences are called "dance."

♪ Songs to sing and sign DANCE

DARK

Place *closed hands* with palms facing in at the sides of the face. Then cross hands in front of face and continue in downward motion until fingertips are near opposite elbows.

Child may cover face with hands.

♪ Tips for teaching the sign for DARK

○ Many children are frightened of the dark, and it is helpful for them to be able to label their fear with a signed word. Show your toddler how to turn on and off the light switch to darken her room as part of your nighttime ritual. Your child may not be alarmed when you turn off the lights in her room, but she may benefit from using the spoken and signed word for DARK to signal that it is time to turn off the lights and say NIGHT-NIGHT (page 114).

○ Explain to her with your signs and spoken words that the DARKNESS helps remind us that it is time for BED (page 34). Show her the MOON (page 105) in the sky, and tell her that the SUN (page 151) must go DOWN (page 68) and DARKEN the sky for the MOON to rise. Using photographs of the moon and sun or looking at picture books helps make these concepts more concrete.

○ Refer to teaching tips given for LIGHT-OFF (page 96) for more ideas.

♪ Song to sing and sign DARK

12. Now I Lay Me Down to Sleep (page 224)

SIGN OF SUCCESS

"I used the light switch in my daughter's bedroom to teach this concept. I signed LIGHT (page 96) when I flipped it on and DARK when I flipped it off. I did this every time I turned the light on and off."

—Darcy B.

DIAPER

see Bedtime Bonus Signs (page 170)

DIG

Both *cupped hands* alternate "digging in dirt" like a dog or rabbit (dig with hands).

Child may use both hands to dig as if imitating a bunny digging.

♪ Tips for teaching the sign for DIG

○ There are special ASL signs for each different meaning of DIG. To simplify teaching the concept of DIG to your child, and because we sing about "John the Rabbit" (page 195) digging in his garden, the DIG sign shown in this book is for digging with hands—or paws. We also know that babies and toddlers dig in the sandbox or rice bin with their hands. If you are digging with a shovel, the ASL sign for DIG looks like a pantomimed version of that action.

○ Digging is a great way to explore new food textures and have fun at the same time. HIDE (page 91) a banana slice at the bottom of a bowl of cereal-Os. Show your child how to use his fingers or a spoon to DIG to the bottom of the bowl to find the treasure! Allow your child to explore new food textures with his fingers as well as his tongue. He is more likely to sample new foods if he is given the freedom to choose how and when the morsel will wind up in his mouth.

○ Plant some vegetables or herbs in a pot and let your child dig in the dirt to sow the seeds. Show him how to DIG with his fingertips or let him use a small cup or scoop to make the hole for the seeds.

♪ Song to sing and sign DIG

5. John the Rabbit (page 195)

♪ Play, Sign, and Learn: DIG

Dig-hetti

Materials:
- Large bowl, deep pan, or a plastic tote with low sides
- Cooked spaghetti
- Olive oil or vegetable oil
- Sand toys: a scoop, a small rake, and a small bucket or bowl
- Tablecloth or shower curtain

Children learn through their senses. Sensory experiences help children learn about the world around them. Exposure to a variety of textures helps promote fine motor development. Dig-hetti is a twist on the traditional bean, rice, or water table experience.

Cook a package of spaghetti until it is "al dente" (still firm but not too soft); then let it cool. Pour the cooked spaghetti into a deep pan or plastic tote and add a few drops of olive oil or vegetable oil. The oil will keep the spaghetti from sticking together. Put the pan on a tablecloth or shower curtain that has been placed on your kitchen floor.

Invite your son to play and dig. Stick your hands in the spaghetti and model how you can dig and play with the long noodles. Sign and say DIG as you tell him that it is his turn to DIG. He may be cautious at first as it is a new sensory experience and it may feel funny to the touch. Model for him how much fun it is to dig in the spaghetti. Use a small toy hand rake or plastic pasta spoon to dig and scoop up the spaghetti and put it in the bucket. Pour it back in and dig some more.

- Be silly. Say, "Look at what I can do when I DIG." Dig in and grab a handful of spaghetti. Hold it under your nose like a mustache or hold it under your ear for an earring. Put some on your head as a wig of hair. Dig and dig.
- Dig and scoop spaghetti in your small bowl or bucket. Get out two bowls and race to see who can dig the fastest and fill their bowl first.
- Dig a hole in the spaghetti and put your hands in the hole. Ask your son to cover up your hands with the spaghetti. Laugh and giggle as he covers your hands. Now trade places. Ask your son to dig a big hole in the spaghetti. Be dramatic as you scoop the spaghetti on his hands to cover them. Dig in and have fun!

Adult supervision is necessary for this activity. The materials for Dig-hetti could pose a choking hazard if swallowed.

DIP

see Mealtime Bonus Signs (page 164)

DIRTY

see Bedtime Bonus Signs (page 170)

DOG

Pat leg with *closed hand* as if calling a dog.

Child may pat one or both legs.

♪ Tips for teaching the sign for DOG

○ Point to a real dog and then sign and say the word DOG. If your child is frightened of dogs, stay at a distance from the canine critter to help your child remain calm and to help her focus on her "dog lesson."

○ Call your child's attention to a variety of dogs with large and small bodies, different colors and textures of fur, and different-sounding barks. Identify them all as DOG for your child. You can also show her photographs, books, or toy dogs when she has seen what real dogs look like first.

○ Toddlers may want to engage in some imaginative play by pretending to be a dog. Show her how to crawl on her hands and knees, make a barking sound, and KISS (page 94) the humans she loves. Ask your child: "What does the DOGGIE say?" With practice, you will likely hear an enthusiastic "Woof!"

♪ Song to sing and sign DOG

1. My Kitchen Door (page 182)

DOLL

see Bedtime Bonus Signs (page 170)

DON'T-LIKE

see Mealtime Bonus Signs (page 164)

DOWN

Move pointer finger in
a downward motion.

Child may move
palm down,
or squat as they
point down.

♪ Tips for teaching the sign for DOWN

○ Utilize the activities of your daily life as a family to teach the DOWN sign: stack blocks from the toy box and knock them down; walk down the stairs or driveway at your house; slide down the slide or scoot down the hill on your bottom at the park. Create a "down, down, down" chant for your activities.

○ Find a cardboard mailing tube and remove the caps from both ends. Show your child how to slide small TOYS (page 126) and objects such as balls and beanie animals DOWN the length of the tube. Position the tube so that your child can see you put the toy in the top of the tube and watch the toy come out on the other end. ***Make sure the toys do not pose a choking hazard for your child.***

○ Refer to teaching tips given for UP (page 156) for more ideas.

♪ Song to sing and sign DOWN

7. Mister Moon (page 204)

DREAM

see Lullaby Bedtime Bonus Signs (page 173)

DRINK

Bring *cupped hand* to lips as if holding a cup.

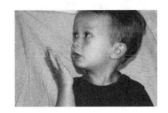

Child may touch mouth with one finger or all fingertips.

♪ Tips for teaching the sign for DRINK

○ Children usually begin transitioning from drinking only from a bottle to drinking also from a cup at around nine months. The same coordination necessary for controlling their hands and mouth to drink from a cup will be utilized as they master fine and oral motor skills to be able to sign and speak.

○ If you are still breast-feeding or giving your child formula, use the sign MILK (page 102) for these "drinks." The DRINK sign can then refer to water or diluted juice that your child drinks from a cup. Give her opportunities to practice drinking from a training cup at each meal and throughout the day.

○ When you have taken your child entirely off bottles or weaned her from breast-feeding, milk becomes another drink option: "What do you want to DRINK with your supper: MILK? WATER? (page 161)?" Some children enjoy drinking from a straw as they transition from a bottle to a cup. Using a straw may also increase their interest in drinking water.

♪ Songs to sing and sign DRINK

3. The Muffin Man (page 188)
6. What Did You Have for Your Supper? (page 200)
10. What'll We Do with the Baby? (page 215)

DRY

Bend pointer finger and then pull it sideways under the chin from one side to the other.

Child may wipe lips or chin with a straight pointer finger.

♪ Tips for teaching the sign for DRY

○ Sensory experience is vital to babies and toddlers, and some children learn best through touch sensations. Involve your child in daily activities that include objects that are wet and dry. Let him help you dry the wet plastic dishes you use for mealtime with a cloth. Show him how to put the wet clothes from the washing machine into the dryer, and have him assist you taking the clothes out of the dryer when they are finished. With each task, be sure to use your DRY sign.

○ The sign for WET (page 172) becomes a useful and motivating sign for your child to use when he is uncomfortable in his wet diaper. Ask him if his DIAPER (page 170) is DRY or DIRTY (page 171). Show him the sign for DRY as you check his diaper. You can also sign DRY PANTS (page 120) for "big boy" pull-ups or underwear, and praise him for staying DRY.

♪ Song to sing and sign DRY

8. We're Having a Bath (page 208)

DUCK

Open and close "duck's bill" next to mouth by tapping thumb to closed pointer and middle fingers.

Child may open and close *gathered fingertips* with or without placing them next to mouth, or place finger or fingers at mouth without making a motion.

♪ Tips for teaching the sign for DUCK

○ DUCK is an easy sign to teach. There is an abundance of duck bath toys, and actual "duckies" are swimming in the pond of your local park or zoo. Take along BREAD (page 40) or CRACKER (page 60) to FEED (page 73) the HUNGRY (page 93) ducks at the park. Make sure you feed them small bites to extend your sign practice.

○ Engage your child in imaginative play and pretend your child is a duck. Toddlers enjoy making the "quack" duck sound as they perform the DUCK sign. Ducks like to waddle in the water of a shallow wading pool. They like to eat crackers and sit in the sunshine with their "duckie mommies." Feed your little duck a CRACKER or a slice of BREAD. Ask for a "quack" to say THANK YOU (page 168)!

♪ Song to sing and sign DUCK

1. My Kitchen Door (page 182)

♪ Play, Sign, and Learn: DUCK

"Duck, Duck, Goose" placemat

Materials
- Computer with Internet access and printer, or magazines and newspapers
- Plastic page protector or laminator

The "Duck, Duck, Goose" game is a favorite with little children. Here is a placemat version perfect for entertaining your toddler while you are preparing a meal for your family. To make your "duck and not duck" placemat for your child, use the Internet search engine of your choice, select "images," and type the word "duck." Find a photograph of a duck that you like; copy and paste two identical duck photographs on a blank page. Then choose another animal or object that your child can sign, such as DOG (page 67), RABBIT (page 132), or FLOWER (page 77). Add this photograph next to your two identical DUCK pictures. You can also cut pictures out of magazines or newspapers to create your placemat. Laminate the page at your local copy store or place it in a clear plastic page protector to extend the life of your placemat.

Show it to your child, and help her point to each object from left to right. Sign the word after you point to each picture. Eventually your child will be able to point to the objects and sign their names while you are saying them for her. Make several variations of this placemat with other sign vocabulary animals and objects you are learning. This is a great way to teach children an early reading skill: tracking objects on a page from left to right. You are also teaching her to recognize when objects are the same and when they are different.

EAT/FOOD/NIBBLE/MEALTIME and FEED (BREAKFAST, LUNCH, SUPPER, SNACK)

Tap *gathered fingertips* to lips.

Direct *gathered fingertips* away from body as if you are giving food to another (FEED).

Child may place *open hand* on or in mouth for EAT signs as well as FEED.

♪ Tips for teaching the signs for EAT and FEED

○ The EAT sign is simple because all that the child needs to do is get his hand to his mouth—right where the food goes in! You can use the FEED sign by telling your child you will feed him when you get home from the park, and place your fingertips on your child's lips. ASL has separate signs for breakfast, lunch, and dinner that use some of the hand shapes of the signed alphabet. For the purpose of this book, the EAT sign will be used for mealtimes as well.

○ Use the EAT sign as you eat and snack and as a choice when you are trying to solve the mystery of why your child is unhappy: "I see you are sad right now. Do you need to SLEEP (page 34)? Do you need to EAT? Do you need a HUG? (page 98)"

○ Refer to teaching tips given for HUNGRY (page 93) or "Sign Solutions" (page 30, 50, and 81) for more ideas and information about EAT.

♪ Songs to sing and sign EAT/FOOD/NIBBLE/MEALTIME and FEED

1. My Kitchen Door (page 182)
2. Crawly, Creepy Little Mousie (page 185)
3. The Muffin Man (page 188)

SIGN OF SUCCESS

"My daughter performed the EAT sign by simply pointing with her index finger to her mouth. She learned this gesture quickly and used it often."

—Amanda F.

FARM

see Lullaby Bonus Signs (page 173)

FAVORITE

see Mealtime Bonus Signs (page 164)

FEED

see EAT (page 73)

FILL

Move palm side of *closed* hand across the thumb side of other fist toward the body.

Child may tap fist with *open* hand or simply make a fist.

♪ Tips for teaching the sign for FILL

○ This sign is simple for a child to perform and is used to show when something is full, such as a cup or a box. It is also used for the action of filling, such as pouring or dumping things into containers. See FULL (bonus sign, page 166) for the sign used when a person is FULL of food or satisfied with the amount they have eaten.

○ Babies and toddlers love to fill things and dump them out again. Fill a plastic tub with a lid full of rice, corn meal, or oatmeal. *Avoid using beans or other items that could pose a choking hazard.* Place the box on a plastic tablecloth or beach towel for easy cleanup. Add cups and spoons for your child to FILL with rice or meal and dump back into the container. Hide some TOYS (page 126) under the mixture so that your child can DIG (page 64) to find them.

○ Mastering the concept of empty and full utilizes simple materials that are readily at hand in your home. Your child can FILL a bag with balls or toys, a box with blocks, a cup with water, a bucket with sand, or her hands with books: "Thank you for HELPING (page 90) me FILL the bucket."

♪ Song to sing and sign FILL

4. Fill the Basket (page 192)

FINE OR ALRIGHT

Place thumb of *open hand* on chest.

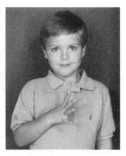

Child may place hand on chest or pat chest with hand.

♪ Tips for teaching the sign for FINE/ALRIGHT

○ Babies can use sign language to tell us why they are unhappy; they can tell us they need SLEEP (page 34), FOOD (page 73), HELP (page 90), SNUGGLES (page 98), or a favorite TOY (page 126). It would be wonderful to give them a word to use when they are just dandy. Here is your word: FINE!

○ Our most common greeting as adults is "Hi! How are you?" And the reply is typically, "Fine." Now you can teach your child how to respond with sign when someone asks them: "How do you do?"

○ The FINE sign can be used to comfort and reassure your child. When you have completed your bedtime rituals and it is time to put your son in his crib, you can say and sign: "Time for NIGHT-NIGHT (page 114). You are FINE. MOMMY (page 104) will see you soon." Using your soothing voice as you pet and pat your child, reassure him that all is well and that you will return in the morning to take him out of his crib as you always do.

♪ Songs to sing and sign FINE/ALRIGHT

3. The Muffin Man (page 188)
8. We're Having a Bath (page 208)
12. Now I Lay Me Down to Sleep (page 224)

FLOWER

Touch tips of *gathered fingertips* on one side of the nose and then the other.

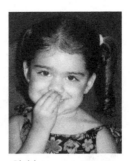

Child may point to nose or touch fingertips to nose and sniff.

♪ Tips for teaching the sign for FLOWER

○ Babies and toddlers love flowers. They are colorful and often smell wonderful. Let your child gently touch the soft petals of a flower and teach her how to smell their scent. Point to all the flowers you see as you take a walk.

○ Pick a flower from your yard—or the yard of a cooperative friend or grandparent—and put it in a cup of WATER (page 161) on your table. Enjoy looking at the flower as you eat your meals. Ask your child to tell someone else at the table about the FLOWER she picked.

○ Visit the FLOWER STORE (page 150) or walk through the floral department of your local grocery store to see lots of flowers in one place. A field trip to a florist shop won't allow your child to experience the flowers by touching, but they may have some blooms to discard that they would happily give to you and your child for your sign language lesson! Make sure to teach the florist the sign for FLOWER.

♪ Songs to sing and sign FLOWER

9. White Sheep and Black Sheep (page 212)
11. Rainbows, Railroads, and Rhymes (page 220)

♪ Play, Sign, and Learn: FLOWER

Spoon Flowers

Materials:
- Small shoebox with lid
- Brown paper
- 12 disposable plastic infant or toddler spoons of various colors
- Permanent marker
- Sharp knife or scissors
- Tape or glue

Colorful flowers catch everyone's eye. Toddlers are especially drawn to the rainbow of colors in a flower garden and have been known to pick one flower too many. By creating a flower garden in a box, your child will have a toddler-friendly flower garden of her own.

Using brown paper (a grocery sack will work well), cover the lid of your shoebox and tape or glue the paper in place. You may cover the entire box if you would like. Next, using a sharp knife or scissors, cut twelve small slits approximately one inch in length in the lid of the box. Make three rows with four slits each. *For safety reasons, it is best to prepare the box without your toddler nearby.* Draw small flowers (petals only) on the bowl-shaped end of the spoons so that the handles of the spoons will serve as the stems. Let your toddler "plant" the flowers in her flower box by placing them in the slits and picking them as she wishes. She will love taking the spoon flowers in and out of the box.

- Count the flowers as your child puts them in and takes them out of the box: "one FLOWER, two FLOWERS . . ." Sign the word FLOWER each time she plants or picks a flower in her box.
- Ask her to pick certain colors and give them to you.
- Put one flower of each color in the back row of the garden box, and then help your toddler sort the spoon flowers by planting them in the matching color row.

All homemade toys require adult supervision and need to be routinely checked to be sure they are safe. The materials for Spoon Flowers could pose a choking hazard if swallowed.

FOOD

see EAT (page 73)

FORK

see Mealtime Bonus Signs (page 164)

FRIEND

Curved pointer fingers
hook, then hook again
in opposite direction.

Child may hook or tap
pointer fingers or fingertips
together without
alternating direction,
or simply place one hand
on top of the other.

♪ Tips for teaching the sign for FRIEND

○ It is important for your child to be around other babies and toddlers their own age.
Don't expect them to share toys as they converse in sign language; at best children this
age will play side by side. This is called parallel play. Use your FRIEND sign to direct
your child's attention to other children. Teach them how to be gentle and kind with
other children just as they are with the petals of FLOWERS (page 77) and the faces and
bodies of their beloved CAT (page 51) or DOG (page 67).

○ Organize a *Sing & Sign* playgroup! Many of the parents in my classes have continued to
meet for playgroups and shared experiences long after our classes have concluded. They
bring along a CD and enjoy their signed songs together. Best of all, parents develop adult
friendships while their children are making new friends.

○ Take pictures of children or caring adult friends of your child. Make him a small "friends" photo album to enjoy. Look at each photograph and identify the person by name. Then sign and say: "He (or she) is your FRIEND. He loves to PLAY (page 126) with you!"

♪ Song to sing and sign FRIEND

4. Fill the Basket (page 192)

FRUIT

Pinched thumb and pointer finger twist forward at cheek.

Child may touch hand or pointer finger to cheek.

♪ Tips for teaching the sign for FRUIT

○ The ability to categorize objects commonly occurs at close to four years of age, so the word FRUIT may be more difficult for a toddler to comprehend than specific words such as APPLE (page 25) and BANANA (page 29). However, the FRUIT sign is included in this book to describe pureed or strained varieties you feed to your baby, less common fruit items you may not know the sign for (such as kiwi or apricot), fruits such as plum that are finger spelled, or items such as fruit cocktail or fruit cups that include more than one type of fruit.

○ It is important to provide a wide variety of fruits to your child within the first two years of her life to keep her from becoming a finicky eater. Introduce a new fruit every week, and model your enthusiasm for each by eating some yourself and saying, "I like this FRUIT!" or "FRUITS are so YUMMY (page 86)!" As she tries each new fruit, she may spit out or turn her head away because of the new taste and texture. Don't become discouraged—eventually she will understand that the foods you label FRUIT are sweet and delicious!

♪ Songs to sing and sign FRUIT

1. My Kitchen Door (page 182)
2. Crawly, Creepy Little Mousie (page 185)
3. The Muffin Man (page 188)
5. John the Rabbit (page 195)

FULL

see Mealtime Bonus Signs (page 164)

SIGN SOLUTIONS: ATTENTION, PLEASE!

Q: *My baby doesn't seem to pay attention to eating at dinnertime. He seems more interested in watching the rest of us eat or in dropping his food on the floor for the dog than in eating. Can sign language help us focus his attention on feeding?*

Overcoming resistance to eating at mealtimes can be accomplished by focusing on the socializing and communication aspects instead. Babies will eat when they are hungry, so keeping the mealtime experience positive regardless of the amount of food eaten is essential. Toddlers do eat sporadically, so it is best to look at what is eaten over an entire week rather than expect each individual meal to be complete.

Your son may have grown accustomed to nestling in your arms in a quiet bedroom to nurse or drink formula from a bottle. As you transition him to a busier location to get his nutrition, he may need some time to get used to this change of venue. He doesn't understand yet that sitting in a high chair in your busy kitchen has something to do with satisfying his hunger. He's too busy watching you prepare a meal for the family, talk on the phone, sing him a song, and make a grocery list all at the same time.

First things first: try to limit distractions in the room where the child eats his meals. Here are a few suggestions:

- Keep the family pet away from your son's chair so he won't be tempted to drop food on the floor. "DOGGIE (page 67) is ALL-DONE (page 23) EATING (page 73). It's your turn to EAT!"

continues

SIGN SOLUTIONS: ATTENTION, PLEASE! *continued*

- Prepare his meal and have it ready before you put him in the high chair. "TIME (page 172) to EAT. Let's sit in your high CHAIR (page 54)."
- Before his meal, try playing outside, taking a walk, or enjoying other games or toys that require his active participation. Other children need activities that calm rather than arouse them before mealtime; perhaps they need to read a book with you, listen to music, or play quietly before their meal. "It is almost time for lunch. Would you like to read a BOOK (page 38) or GO (page 85) outside?" You know your child best; look to see if there is a relationship between his ability to focus on eating and the kinds of activities you and he have enjoyed just before mealtime.
- Develop a mealtime routine that works for the whole family so that you can share at least one meal each day.

Mealtime is one of the most important early social experiences your child enjoys. Sitting together and eating, you are starting to teach him manners—"MORE (page 107) PEAS (page 123), PLEASE (page 127)"—and conversational skills. Talk about your plans for the day, about play activities or people that interest your child, or about what a fabulous job he is doing trying new foods.

A Washington University researcher, Diane Beals, Ed.D., found that families who eat meals together improved the language skills of their young children. Young children who were exposed to "rare" words as a part of mealtime conversation had larger vocabularies at age five than young children who did not have the same level of exposure. Increased vocabulary is also linked to the child's ability to learn to read.

"Rare," or unusual, words are those that most preschoolers do not know, such as "boxer," "tackling," or "wriggle." Because mealtime conversations tend to be longer, families can talk about anything that interests them, including the names of all the different FLOWERS (page 77) they saw at the PARK (page 174) that day, or how to make the child's favorite MUFFIN (page 109). According to Beals, "There's a broad range of topics that can come up at mealtimes that wouldn't necessarily be introduced in other kinds of settings. . . . It's a very interesting, juicy place to get stories, explanations, and discussions about words."

GIRL

Drag thumb of
closed fist down jaw.

Child may draw fingertips
down jaw or press thumb
against cheek.

♪ Tips for teaching the sign for GIRL

○ Call your daughter your "sweet little GIRL" or refer to her as MOMMY's (page 104) GIRL or DADDY's (page 61) GIRL. Playfully teach her to sign GIRL each time you ask: "Who is sitting in that CHAIR (page 54)?" or "Who is sleeping in that BED (page 34)?" Your child must figure out whether they are a boy or a girl before they can begin to differentiate between the two genders with other children.

○ Make a book of your own called *My Girl*. Take pictures of your daughter during your daily routine together: eating, playing, napping, clapping, and dancing. Put them in a photo album or paste them onto paper and cover the paper with contact paper. Repeat the words "my GIRL" with each page as you describe what your daughter is doing in the photograph, for example, "my GIRL PLAYS (page 126) with toys."

○ Refer to teaching tips given for BOY (page 39) for more ideas.

♪ Song to sing and sign GIRL

1. My Kitchen Door (page 182)

GIVE

Both hands with *gathered fingertips* and palms up extend forward from body with one slightly in front of the other.

Child may push both fists away from body as if holding an object.

♪ Tips for teaching the sign for GIVE

○ If you ask, "Please GIVE me the book," and she hands it to you, she has mastered the meaning of GIVING! Now it's time to teach her to use it to express her desire for something she wants. Encourage her to "tell me with your words" for you to GIVE her the TOY (page 126). She can also assist you with tasks such as GIVING the DOG (page 67) his dry FOOD (page 73), GIVING her breakfast PLATE (page 167) to you when she has finished eating, and GIVING her PAJAMAS (page 119) to you to WASH (page 31) for her.

○ Praise your child's generosity. Thank her every time she purposefully gives you something you haven't requested. Babies and toddlers are seldom capable of willingly sharing the things they treasure and should not be expected to do so. So in those random and infrequent moments when they give a piece of their MUFFIN (page 109) to you, be grateful—and gobble it right up.

♪ Songs to sing and sign GIVE

1. My Kitchen Door (page 182)
10. What'll We Do with the Baby? (page 215)

GO

Extend pointers upward
and then swing them away
from the body with one
slightly in front of the other.

Child may rotate pointer fingers
or whole hands in circular
motion without movement
away from the body.

♪ Tips for teaching the sign for GO

○ Most babies love to GO! They enjoy visits to the STORE (page 150), GRANDPA's (page 174) house, the PARK (page 174), and church. The GO sign will be a simple one for your child to perform: he simply points outside.

○ Use the GO sign to communicate with your child that you will go just as soon as you EAT (page 73), put on SHOES (page 138), and BRUSH-TEETH (page 42), or whatever the necessary steps are in your routine. As you complete each task, encourage your child to sign with you ALL-DONE EAT, ALL-DONE SHOES, and so on. You help eliminate toddler meltdowns when they can anticipate what comes next.

○ Refer to teaching tips for WALK (page 159) for more ideas.

♪ Song to sing and sign GO

9. White Sheep and Black Sheep (page 212)

GOOD OR YUMMY

Place fingertips of *closed hand* to lips. Then, pull hand down and away from lips to rest on palm of other *closed hand*.

Child may pull hand down from mouth.

♪ Tips for teaching the sign for GOOD/YUMMY

○ Babies are born knowing how to use their mouths to self-calm and to learn about their environment. All children respond differently to varying food textures, temperatures, and tastes. You can help your child expand her repertoire of foods by sharing new foods with her often within her first two years of life. When she makes a "yummy" sound or opens her mouth for MORE (page 107), tell her: "The PEAS (page 123) you are eating are YUMMY! I bet you want some MORE."

○ Most pets are not picky eaters. As they gobble their supper time chow, comment to your child about how Scruffy likes his FOOD (page 73) and thinks it is YUMMY.

○ Refer to teaching tips given for BAD/YUCKY (page 28) for more ideas.

♪ Song to sing and sign GOOD/YUMMY

3. The Muffin Man (page 188)

Play, Sign, and Learn: GOOD/YUMMY

A Gift of Good and Yummy

Materials:

- Plain sugar cookies (homemade or from your favorite bakery)
- Frosting (homemade or store-bought cans or tubes)
- Bottles of sprinkles and colored sugar
- Tablecloth
- Paper plates
- Plastic wrap
- Bows

Fred Rogers, the host of *Mr. Rogers' Neighborhood,* encouraged parents to "create a tradition of giving with your children." This activity, inspired by his book *The Giving Box: Create a Tradition of Giving with Your Children* (see "References and Resources," page 271), will help you do just that. The act of sharing food with others is a way of bonding. It will demonstrate to your child the importance of giving and establishing relationships with others.

First, spread out your tablecloth. Assist your child in creating beautiful cookies to share with your neighbors. Talk about the COOKIES (page 165) and how good or yummy they will be. "These COOKIES look so YUMMY!," "Wow, your COOKIE looks so GOOD!" After decorating several cookies, stop and enjoy one yourself. Add extra frosting and sprinkles; you deserve it. While you enjoy your cookie, talk about who will receive them. Do you know them well? Do you think they will like your cookies?

After all of your cookies are decorated, help your child put a few cookies on each paper plate. Now's it's time to package and deliver. You will want to cover the cookies with plastic wrap to keep them fresh and prevent them from falling off the plate. But first, have your daughter decorate your package by placing a bow on the plastic wrap *before* you put it over the cookies. This prevents cookies from being enthusiastically smashed by your "bow assistant."

Before you leave to deliver your cookies, talk to your child about what you will do. Talk about knocking on the doors and ringing doorbells. Practice how you both will say and sign "YUMMY COOKIES" when your neighbor answers the door. Carefully put your plates of cookies in a wagon and set out for delivery to FRIENDS (page 79) old and new.

GRANDMA

see Lullaby Bonus Signs (page 173)

GRANDPA

see Lullaby Bonus Signs (page 173)

GRAPES

Fingertips of open *cupped hand* tap several times on the top of other hand starting near wrist and moving to fingers.

Child may tap palm on top of other hand.

♪ Tips for teaching the sign for GRAPES

○ *Grapes are a great finger food for toddlers as long as they are cut into pieces so that they do not pose a choking hazard.* Offer grapes as a snack choice for picnics and times when you will be on the go: "We're going to the PARK (page 174) today. Do you want me to bring GRAPES or APPLESAUCE (page 25)?"

○ Point grapes out to your child at home, on the salad bar, at the grocery store. Toddlers enjoy talking about the different colors and sizes of grapes as they begin to notice differences and similarities in familiar objects.

♪ Song to sing and sign GRAPES

4. Fill the Basket (page 192)

HAPPY

Open hands brush upward on chest several times.

Child may pat chest with hands.

♪ Tips for teaching the sign for HAPPY

○ When you sign HAPPY, smile from ear to ear. Teaching a hearing or deaf child to sign requires that they learn to pay attention to your facial expression as well as your hands and voice. It is also a good idea for your child to learn to "read" your face and know when you are happy, sad, angry, or frightened.

○ Call your child's attention to HAPPY and SAD faces you see in picture books. Ask her to point to the faces that are HAPPY or SAD on the pages.

○ Refer to teaching tips for SMILE (page 141) for more ideas.

♪ Songs to sing and sign HAPPY

7. Mister Moon (page 204)
8. We're Having a Bath (page 208)

HELP

Place *closed fist* with
thumb extended on other
upward palm. Lift both hands
together as if bottom hand
is lifting the other.

Child may lift hands
with palms facing,
or tap palm with fist.

♪ Tips for teaching the sign for HELP

○ The HELP sign may take children a while to master because their hands must "cooperate" to perform the sign by placing one under the other and lifting. The concept of need-
ing or offering help is also difficult for a young child to grasp. He knows he is frustrated
but doesn't understand what causes him to feel this way. However, once he grasps the relationship between asking for HELP and having his needs met, he will be able to general-
ize its use to every context in his daily life where he needs you to lend him a hand.

○ When your child is obviously trying to accomplish something on his own and could use
your assistance, ask him: "Do you need my HELP? Use your words and tell me what you
need." If he isn't able to perform the sign without assistance, help him form the sign himself with your hands on his.

○ Enlist your child's assistance in tasks around your house; ask him for HELP bringing
his PLATE (page 167) and CUP (page 165) to you, pulling the clothes out of the dryer,
putting TOYS (page 126) in the toy box, making MUFFINS (page 109) for GRANDMA's
(page 174) visit.

♪ Song to sing and sign HELP

2. Crawly, Creepy Little Mousie (page 185)

HIDE

Closed fist of one hand with thumb extended "hides" under other *cupped hand.*

Child may place one hand over the other, similar to her TURTLE sign.

♪ Tips for teaching the sign for HIDE

○ Children love things that are hidden and then found. "Peek-a-Boo" is often your baby's first game and a guaranteed opportunity to see her smile. To modify this familiar chant, say: "Peek-a-Boo, I'm HIDING from you!" and sign the word HIDE.

○ Show your baby a desirable toy and then cover it up with a blanket. If your baby reaches for the blanket instead of looking sad or confused, you can begin playing "hide the toy" in earnest. Developmental psychologist Jean Piaget used this experiment and determined that by eight or nine months of age, babies discover that toys continue to exist even when they are out of sight. Other researchers have found that babies learn this as young as three months.

○ Use the HIDE sign as you locate familiar items—SHOE (page 138), TOOTHBRUSH (page 42), BANANA (page 29)—and ask your child where it is: "Where is your SHOE? Is it HIDING? Oh, there it is!"

♪ Songs to sing and sign HIDE

5. John the Rabbit (page 195)
7. Mister Moon (page 204)

HOLD

see LOVE (page 98)

HOME

Touch *gathered fingertips* near mouth. Then move them to cheek by the ear.

Child may tap fingers to cheek.

♪ Tips for teaching the sign for HOME

○ Home is a place of comfort and security for your child, where all of his favorite foods and toys are stored. Giving your child a sign for HOME enables him to anticipate his return to this favorite place. As you finish your grocery shopping, you can promise him: "We will go HOME just as soon as we are ALL-DONE (page 23) at the STORE (page 150)."

○ Make up a song to a familiar tune such as "The Farmer in the Dell" about going home. Sing: "We're going to our HOME, we're going to the HOME, hey-ho, my baby-oh, we're going to our HOME." Sing it all the way to the driveway! When you stop the car, sing your child a new verse: "We've made it to our HOME . . . "

○ One of the first toys we purchased was a toy house with little plastic people made especially for babies. Talk to your child about the toy version of his HOME and the people who live inside: MOMMY (page 104), DADDY (page 61), SISTER (page 175), and BROTHER (page 173).

♪ Song to sing and sign HOME

9. White Sheep and Black Sheep (page 212)

HOT

see Mealtime Bonus Signs (page 164)

HUG

see LOVE (page 98)

HUNGRY

Pull *cupped hand* down chest.

Child may pull hand down chest or point to tummy.

♪ Tips for teaching the sign for HUNGRY

○ Teaching the sign for HUNGER requires that you teach your child to recognize and label a feeling or sensation called hunger. Children usually become uncomfortable or unhappy when it is time to eat, but they aren't able to articulate what is troubling them. If you provide meals and snacks for your child at regular and predictable intervals, it will be easier for you to observe when she is ready to eat. Pair your HUNGER sign with the sign for EAT/FOOD (page 73): "You look HUNGRY. Do you want FOOD?" Giving your child food after you sign HUNGRY will also help her make the connection between the two.

○ Share a snack with your toddler. Begin by signing and saying: "I am HUNGRY. I need FOOD." Eat some of the snack you have prepared. Next, ask your child: "Are you HUNGRY?" Then give her a portion of the snack food as well.

○ Refer to teaching tips given for EAT and "Sign Solutions" (page 30, 50, and 81) for more ideas and information about HUNGRY.

♪ Songs to sing and sign for HUNGRY

    1. My Kitchen Door (page 182)
    3. The Muffin Man (page 188)

ICE CREAM

see Mealtime Bonus Signs (page 164)

JUICE

see Mealtime Bonus Signs (page 164)

KISS

Touch mouth with pointer finger. Then tap *gathered fingertips* of both hands together.

Child may touch lips while puckering lips.

♪ Tips for teaching the sign for KISS

○ KISS is a wonderful sign to practice with your child! Show him the sign and then give him a kiss. You can kiss your sweet boy, kiss his stuffed animals, or "babies," or kiss your spouse.

○ Boo-boos get better much faster when you give them a kiss: "Do you WANT (page 160) me to KISS your boo-boo?"

○ Blow kisses to the people your child loves. Your child can blow MOMMY (page 104) or DADDY (page 61) a kiss if they leave for work in the morning. Make blowing him a kiss a part of your bedtime routine.

♪ Songs to sing and sign for KISS

10. What'll We Do with the Baby? (page 215)
11. Rainbows, Railroads, and Rhymes (page 220)

♪ Play, Sign, and Learn: KISS

A Kiss Good Night

"A kiss goodnight with a hug real tight is nothing short of bliss."
—FRANK SINATRA, "A KISS GOOD NIGHT"

Between the ages of eighteen and twenty-four months, children begin to demonstrate simple pretend play. They imitate actions they observe and take on the roles of those most familiar to them. They pretend to drink from a cup and talk on a play telephone. Our hearts swell the first time we observe our children taking care of and loving their "babies" and stuffed animals. When children feed their "babies" and give them kisses, they are taking on the role of caretaker for them.

Research tells us pretend, or dramatic, play is a necessary stage in development. It is an essential building block of cognition, and social, emotional, and language skills. Ellen Booth Church, a former professor of early childhood education, an education consultant, and an author, shares that "when your child engages in pretend (or dramatic) play, he is actively experimenting with the social and emotional roles of life" (see "References and Resources," page 271). When your child pretends to be different characters, he has the experience of "walking in someone else's shoes," which helps teach the important moral development skill of empathy.

You can foster pretend play with your child by creating opportunities for imaginative play and modeling it when you play with your child. You can become an animal and crawl on all fours, you can be a chef and make delicious food, and you can be a mommy or daddy to your child's babies and animals. Talk to your child's babies and animals as if they are real. Model a bedtime routine for the babies and animals. "It's time for NIGHT-NIGHT (page 114), baby. Let me give you a HUG (page 98) and a KISS." Continue this routine with some of the stuffed animals, too. Hand an animal to your son. Tell him, "KISS hippo good night. He is SLEEPY (page 34)." You may even want to consider adding this play sequence into your child's bedtime routine. By creating a bedtime experience for his babies and stuffed animals, your son may be able to better prepare himself for his own bedtime routine.

Your child will appreciate a consistent bedtime routine. Children relax knowing what to expect and develop better sleep habits as a result. Evaluate your child's bedtime routine. Is it predictable and consistent? Regardless of the steps, saying good night is complete with a hug and a kiss. Through your imaginative play and through real bedtime experiences, a kiss goodnight has many benefits.

LIGHT OR LIGHT-OFF

Pointer finger circles above head, then forms *gathered fingertips* that move to *cupped open hand* palm (LIGHT). *Cupped open hand* palm down changes to *gathered fingertips* while arm is extended above head (LIGHT-OFF).

Child may open and close fingers repeatedly for both LIGHT and LIGHT-OFF.

♪ Tips for teaching the sign for LIGHT

○ Call your child's attention to lights in her world both in your house and as you travel. Your baby needs to know all the different bright objects we call LIGHT before she can determine whether they are on or off. Sign LIGHT as you point them out to her.

○ Arrange some of your child's favorite toys or other objects on the floor, shelf, or windowsill in her room. Lay with your heads on a pillow on the floor or in her bed. Turn on the flashlight and hand it to her for her to hold; then sign and say LIGHT. Show her how to point to her favorite toys with the beam of light. Make a game of asking her to point her LIGHT at BEAR (page 32), TOY (page 126), or SHOE (page 138).

○ Turn the LIGHT OFF intermittently throughout the day and spend some time SNUGGLING (page 98) and loving your child in the DARK (page 63). She will learn that darkness can be a safe and comforting place in your presence and perhaps learn how to comfort herself with these warm memories when the light is out.

○ Refer to teaching tips given for DARK for more ideas.

♪ Songs to sing and sign LIGHT

7. Mister Moon (page 204)
9. White Sheep and Black Sheep (page 212)
11. Railroads, Rainbows, and Rhymes (page 220)

LIKE

see Mealtime Bonus Signs (page 164)

LITTLE

see Mealtime Bonus Signs (page 164)

LOTION

see Bedtime Bonus Signs (page 170)

LOVE OR HOLD OR HUG OR SNUGGLE

Place both *open hands* across chest and squeeze arms as if hugging self (HUG). Place both *closed fists* across chest (LOVE). HOLD and SNUGGLE are signs similar to LOVE when referring to nurturing another person.

Child will likely hug self.

♪ Tips for teaching the sign for LOVE/HOLD/HUG/SNUGGLE

○ No lesson is more important to teach your child than to LOVE and receive LOVE from others. The best way to teach the sign for LOVE is to wrap your arms around your child and gently squeeze him as you say "I LOVE you," adding emphasis to the spoken and signed word LOVE with a slightly tighter hug.

○ Just as you instruct your child in proper manners by teaching him to say "please," "thank you," and "sorry," teach your child to show affection to others. Ask your child to give LOVE or a HUG to family members or friends if your child has a close personal friendship with that person.

○ Model affection in your child's presence. Let him observe you hug your spouse, your parents, a close friend. Tell these people you LOVE them with your hands, your voice, and your actions. Look at their face, smile at them, touch them, laugh with them. Let your child learn how to love others by your example.

♪ Songs to sing and sign LOVE/HOLD/HUG/SNUGGLE

3. The Muffin Man (page 188)
6. What Did You Have for Your Supper? (page 200)

SIGN SOLUTIONS:
MY BABY IS SINGING THE BEDTIME BLUES

Q: *Getting my child to fall asleep is really difficult. She gets so upset that most of the time I end up in tears as well. Can sign language be of any help with our bedtime battles?*

Without a doubt, sleeping issues weigh heavily on parent's minds. What is right for one family may not work well for another. The National Sleep Foundation's report "Sleep in America Poll" showed that seventy-six percent of parents have sleeping-related issues that they would like to change. Children's sleep problems cause stress and sleep deprivation in caregivers.

Your baby likes you, and you cannot blame baby one bit for wanting to continue to party with you rather than go to bed. However, your baby needs proper rest to think, grow, and participate happily as a member of your family. Getting enough sleep is also important for good health. Many parents may not know the recommended amount of sleep required for different ages. In a twenty-four-hour period, newborns require sixteen–twenty hours, infants thirteen–fifteen, toddlers twelve, preschoolers eleven–twelve hours, and older children ten–eleven hours.

Here are some tips for incorporating pediatrician-approved strategies with sign language and music to help your child go to sleep:

- It is important to keep the crib clear of a lot of stuffed animals, pillows, and other distractions. One transition object, such as their blanket or a favorite stuffed animal, works best. Children may also associate sleep with the degree of light in the room. Whatever is provided at bedtime must also be there for normal nighttime arousals as well for the baby to get back to sleep on his own. What is your child's light preference: LIGHT-OFF or perhaps a soft night light? Can your child use his sign vocabulary to request his light preference or ask for his preferred transition object?

continues

SIGN SOLUTIONS: MY BABY IS SINGING THE BEDTIME BLUES *continued*

- Separation anxiety can lead to bedtime resistance. If the baby is six–eight months old, parents can begin "letting the baby cry" at bedtime after the already established bedtime routine has been carried out. The caregiver should appear in the room at ten- to twenty-minute intervals to reassure the baby. The caregiver should not pick up the child. Signing with a pat on the back or reassuring touch should be provided. If this routine is consistently followed, the baby will know the caregiver is there, crying will not lead to being picked up, and the baby can then use his transition object and get himself back to sleep. Patience and consistency are very important here. Babies learn quickly to manipulate with crying. Tell baby he is FINE (page 76) and you will see him in the morning.
- Make the effort to set up a consistent and predictable bedtime routine for children between three and nine months of age. This is a critical window of opportunity for you to establish good sleep habits for your child. Babies and toddlers are creatures of habit. Like the rest of us, they like to believe they have some control of their little lives. Create a bedtime routine that works for you. Allow the proper amount of time it takes for you and your child to bond and prepare for a peaceful NIGHT-NIGHT (page 114) for you both. Label each step of your bedtime routine with a signed word: BATH (page 31), a bedtime snack (EAT, page 73), BOOKS (page 38), MUSIC (page 111), and DANCING (page 62). Always conclude with LOVE (page 98) in multiple forms—hugs, kisses, spoken reassurances, and the signed word as well. Utilize the lullabies on the *Mealtime and Bedtime Sing & Sign* CD as part of your bedtime routine to help your child transition to slumber.

LUNCH

see EAT (page 73)

MACARONI

see NOODLE (page 116)

MASSAGE

see Bedtime Bonus Signs (page 170)

MEALTIME

see EAT (page 73)

MEAT

Thumb and pointer finger
pinch the space between
thumb and pointer finger
of other *closed hand.*

Child may use one
hand to grab the fingers
of the other.

♪ Tips for teaching the sign for MEAT

○ Parents typically begin offering pureed or finely chopped meats to their children at around nine months, when their child has developed front teeth. The nutrients, calories, and healthy fats found in meat are important for baby's development. Small pieces of meats can be introduced when the child is able to eat finger foods such as mashed or chunked fruits and vegetables. ***However, hot dogs and meat sticks should be avoided; they pose a choking threat to young children.*** Praise her for eating many different foods: "You tried a new MEAT today. You are so big!"

○ Explain to your child that your pet eats food made of MEAT. Make a story about how much your DOG (page 67) or CAT (page 51) likes to eat MEAT. In your best Dr. Seuss *Green Eggs and Ham* imitation (see "Sing and Sign—and Read—with Picture Books," page 247), tell your boy about how your dog or cat likes to eat MEAT with a SPOON (page 168), he likes to eat MEAT under the MOON (page 105), he likes to eat MEAT in his PAJAMAS (page 119), he likes to eat MEAT with his GRANDMA (page 174), and so on. Rhyming isn't a requirement, but silliness is! And hearing rhyming words supports early reading skills.

♪ Songs to sing and sign MEAT

SIGN OF SUCCESS

"My son wasn't very interested in trying MEAT until I ate it in front of him and signed the word along with YUMMY (page 86) and WANT (page 160). I was very theatrical and exaggerated with my signs. My son thought this was very funny and tried meat as part of the 'game.' MEAT is now a sign he uses to request this food."

—Kim I.

MILK ☀

Repeatedly squeeze one *closed fist* as if milking a cow.

Child may open and close hand several times.

♪ Tips for teaching the sign for MILK

○ Milk is the primary source of nutrition—whether formula or breast milk—during the first year of a child's life, so it is a frequently requested and motivating word for children to learn. The sign for MILK is easy to perform, as it uses a whole hand shape. After the child can imitate a closed fist, he is able to sign MILK.

○ Some parents like to reserve the MILK sign for cow's milk or formula that their child drinks from a cup or bottle. Others prefer to use the MILK sign for all types of milk their child receives: breast milk or cow's milk and formula from a cup or a bottle.

○ Many parents report that their babies sign MILK while they nurse, and this is an especially meaningful and precious sign language experience for them. If you want, you can use a different sign for breast-feeding to distinguish this experience from drinking milk from a bottle or a cup. BREASTFEED is signed by patting one *closed hand* on your upper chest.

♪ Songs to sing and sign MILK

1. My Kitchen Door (page 182)
3. The Muffin Man (page 188)

SIGN OF SUCCESS

"Our daughter learned the milk sign as she was looking at her word picture book. Whenever we showed her the picture of milk, we signed it as we said it. After about a week, she started to do the sign on her own when she saw the picture in her book. The day she signed MILK with the picture is the same day she signed it when she wanted milk. If we don't respond quickly to her sign, she goes to the refrigerator so that we know exactly what she means. This has been one of the most helpful signs for our family. She now usually says the word as she signs it."
—Wendee E.

MINE

see Mealtime Bonus Signs (page 164)

MOMMY

Place thumb of
open hand on chin.

Child may point to her
chin or place fingertips or
palm on chin or cheek.

♪ Tips for teaching the sign for MOMMY

○ MOMMY is not always a sign children choose to use. They certainly know who mommy is; they just don't have a need to ask for her if she is always close at hand. "Mama" and "Dada" are also words children are able to speak at a fairly early age. The sign is also difficult for some children to perform because it requires them to find their chin with their thumb. To help your child with this motion, sign MOMMY for her and then touch your thumb to her chin as you say MOMMY. Do this several times so that she feels where she should place her thumb on her own face.

○ Enlist family members or caregivers in signing MOMMY (or DADDY, page 61) for your child in your absence. If you are gone to the store for an hour or work outside the home each day, the caring adults in your child's life can reassure her that MOMMY will be back soon, and that MOMMY is thinking about her little girl and LOVES (page 98) her. Leave a photograph so that the connection between the word MOMMY and the important lady in the picture can be reinforced by your caregiver or relative.

○ Refer to teaching tips for DADDY for more ideas.

♪ Songs to sing and sign MOMMY

6. What Did You Have for Your Supper? (page 200)
11. Rainbows, Railroads, and Rhymes (page 220)
12. Now I Lay Me Down to Sleep (page 224)

MOON

Lift curved pointer
finger and thumb from
eye in upward motion.

Child may simply
lift hand over head.

♪ Tips for teaching the sign for MOON

○ Use signed vocabulary words your child knows to a describe the moon; it looks like a PLATE (page 167), CHEESE (page 55), or sometimes a SMILING (page 141) face. Talk about how the moon is UP (page 156) in the sky at NIGHT-NIGHT (page 114). In the morning my son would explain the moon's absence by signing with great authority: MOON DOWN (page 68)!

○ Bring the moon indoors by making a picture of it for your child's bedroom. All you need are sheets of black and white construction paper, scissors, and glue. Cut out a large white circle and paste it to the black sheet of paper. Fasten your child's "moon" to a bulletin board or wall in his room so that he can see it. Play a flashlight game (see LIGHT-OFF, page 96) and show your child how to point the beam of the flashlight at "his moon." You can also create a yellow "sun" for your child's room and make taking one picture down and putting the other up a part of your morning and bedtime rituals.

♪ Song to sing and sign MOON

7. Mister Moon (page 204)

♪ Play, Sign, and Learn: MOON

Hide the Moon, Alice!

Materials:
- White plastic lid or cardboard circle

Children are fascinated with hiding and finding things. "Hide and Seek" is a game that has been enjoyed by babies and their families for generations. Another common source of wonder—for both young and old alike—is the moon. To play "Hide the Moon, Alice!" one person will hide the moon and another will find it. To create your "moon," simply draw a crescent moon shape on a plastic lid or cardboard circle. To teach the game, show the moon to your toddler. Tell him that you are going to hide it. Have him close and cover his eyes while you hide the moon in an easily accessible location. Tell him when you are ready for him to find the moon. As your child begins to hunt for the moon, chant or sing these words to the tune of "Mister Moon" (page 204):

> "Little MOON, MOON,
> Bright and shiny MOON,
> Where are you HIDING (page 91) from me?
> Little MOON, MOON,
> Bright and shiny MOON,
> WHERE (page 162), oh WHERE can you be?"

You can even make up more verses by singing phrases such as "Are you under the pillow or behind the CHAIR (page 54)?" This is a great way to introduce prepositions into your toddler's vocabulary. When your toddler finds the moon, say, "Great job! You found the MOON. It was _____." (State the location: under the chair, on the table, and so on.) Then say, "It must be time to SLEEP (page 34). NIGHT-NIGHT (page 114)." Then, lie down on the floor and pretend to sleep. After a few seconds pass, call out "WAKE (page 172) up!" Pretend to wake from a long sleep by yawning and stretching. Now it's your toddler's turn to hide the moon.

MORE

Tap tips of *gathered fingertips* of both hands together several times.

Child may bring pointer finger or several fingertips of one hand to palm of other *open hand* or touch fingertips of both *open hands* together.

♪ Tips for teaching the sign for MORE

○ The sign for MORE is certainly the most popular baby sign, and for good reason: it helps children get their basic needs met. Your child can sign MORE to let you know she wants more FOOD (page 73), TOYS (page 126), DOG (page 67), BOOKS (page 38), and HUGS (page 98). The list goes on.

○ Because so much of baby's attention is centered on being HUNGRY (page 93) and EATING (page 73), she most often uses the MORE sign to let you know she wants more food. She may sign MORE to tell you she wants something she hasn't already received. For instance, she may crawl to your pantry and start to sign MORE because she is hungry and wants a snack. Babies often use the MORE sign at first to communicate "I am telling you I need something. Now it is your turn to figure out what I need." As she learns more signs, she will become more precise in their usage, perhaps signing instead: HUNGRY or FOOD PLEASE (page 127).

♪ Songs to sing and sign MORE

1. My Kitchen Door (page 182)
4. Fill the Basket (page 192)
5. John the Rabbit (page 195)

MOUSE

Brush one pointer finger across the tip of nose several times.

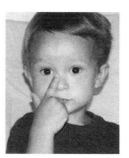

Child may place or tap pointer finger on nose.

♪ Tips for teaching the sign for MOUSE

○ The finger brush of the nose in the MOUSE sign pantomimes the mouse's twitching nose. You can pair teaching this sign with "WHERE (page 162) is the MOUSIE'S nose?" Your child may like to look at mice from the safety of your arms at your local pet store or photographs of them in picture books.

○ Your child might like to pretend to be a mouse and have a CHEESE snack of his own. Add a soft rope or bathrobe sash to your toddler's waist so your little "mouse" has a tail. Can your toddler "mouse" crawl? Can he crawl or run from MOMMY (page 104) CAT (page 51)? Can he HIDE (page 91) from her? Can MOMMY CAT and little MOUSE become FRIENDS (page 79)?

♪ Songs to sing and sign MOUSE

1. My Kitchen Door (page 182)
2. Crawly, Creepy Little Mousie (page 185)

MUFFIN

Cupped fingertips of one hand tap and lift off other upturned palm.

Child may place palm or fingertips of one hand on other hand.

♪ Tips for teaching the sign for MUFFIN

○ The ASL sign for MUFFIN is the same one used for CAKE (page 165). Add pureed or diced fruit to your muffin recipe to make your muffins tasty as well as healthy. Some children may be allergic to foods made with wheat; it is recommended that parents wait until their child is at least eight months old before offering him a food made with wheat.

○ Create your own story loosely based on *If You Give a Moose a Muffin* ("Sing and Sign—and Read—with Picture Books," page 247). Instead, tell your child a tale about giving her a muffin. Then ask her what she would like to eat or drink next after she munched a muffin: MILK or WATER? CHEESE or MEAT? GRAPES or BANANA? You can make flash cards of different signed food vocabulary words your child has learned. Show your child two choices, and let her pick one by saying or signing her choice. Place them in order from left to right on the floor, high chair, or table. When your child has finished making her choices, tell her the story again in the order you have created: "If you give Sarah a MUFFIN, she will probably want some MILK. If you give Sarah some MILK, she will probably want some CHEESE," and so on, until you have finished all the cards in the row. You can collect the picture cards as you "read" each one in order. Using pictures to create meaning is a wonderful pre-reading skill, and the best part of all is that your child has participated in creating the story.

♪ Song to sing and sign MUFFIN

3. The Muffin Man (page 188)

♪ Play, Sign, and Learn: MUFFIN

Muffins Anyone?

If your child enjoys being with you while you are baking or shows an interest in helping you cook, muffins are a great item to make together. They taste delicious, they are easy to make, and they only take a short time to bake. Ask your child if she wants to help you make muffins. Then say: "We can make MUFFINS just like the Muffin Man." Sing "The Muffin Man" as you mix up this fun treat.

Whole Grain Muffins

2 cups Aunt Jemima® Whole
    Wheat Pancake & Waffle Mix
1/2 tsp. ground cinnamon
2/3 cup 2% milk
1/3 cup honey
1 egg, slightly beaten
1/4 cup vegetable oil
1 tsp. vanilla extract

Servings: 12

- Preheat oven to 425 degrees Fahrenheit.
- Spray 12 medium muffin cups with nonfat cooking spray or line with paper baking cups.
- Combine pancake mix and cinnamon in medium bowl.
- Combine milk, honey, egg, oil, and vanilla in small bowl with wire whisk; add to dry mixture. Mix just until dry ingredients are moistened.
- Fill muffin cups 3/4 full. Bake 15–18 minutes or until toothpick inserted in center comes out clean.
- Cool 2 minutes in pan. Remove to cooling rack.

(Copyright © by the Quaker Oats Company. Reprinted with permission.)

All cooking activities require adult supervision. It is important to note that children under the age of one should not have raw honey. Keep this in mind as you mix the ingredients for this recipe. Have your child assist with all of the ingredients except the raw honey and raw egg. Also, do not let your child taste the batter. Wait for the yummy muffins to be baked.

MUSIC OR SING OR SONG

Wave the palm of one *closed hand* over the other extended arm. Sweep hand back and forth from wrist to shoulder.

Child may wave one or both arms at her sides.

♪ Tips for teaching the sign for MUSIC/SING/SONG

○ The sign for MUSIC is one of the first I teach in my *Sing & Sign* classes. It is truly amazing how much music means to young children, second only to eating and snuggling with you. Music then becomes the teaching strategy for learning and practicing signs as well as the reward for performing the signs: "Good signing MUSIC! We will sing MORE (page 107) now!"

○ The MUSIC sign is performed by crossing the body to "conduct" music on one arm with the other waving hand. However, your child may not be able to cross one of his hands over his middle to imitate a sign, or he may do different motions on either side of his body. He will likely sign MUSIC by joyfully and energetically waving his hands in the air. Look for this "sign" and praise your child for saying MUSIC with his hands.

♪ Songs to sing and sign MUSIC/SING/SONG

4. Fill the Basket (page 192)
5. John the Rabbit (page 195)
6. What Did You Have for Your Supper? (page 200)
10. What'll We Do with the Baby? (page 215)
11. Rainbows, Railroads, and Rhymes (page 220)

♪ Play, Sign, and Learn: MUSIC

Mr. Music Please

Abundant research supports the importance of music in the lives of young children. Musical experience promotes language development, social skills, creativity, and much more. Children learn new vocabulary, movement skills, rhythm, and relaxation through their interaction with music. Most importantly, children enjoy music. They enjoy it as passive listeners as well as active participants. Challenge yourself to explore your community for a variety of musical opportunities to enjoy with your child. He will love sharing these musical outings with you and will cherish the musical memories you create together.

Here are a few ideas for your musical excursions. Say and sign MUSIC each time you discover a new musical experience together.

- Check with your local library for special musical events for children.

- Contact your local convention and visitor's bureau for an event calendar—look for festivals that include live music experiences.
- Shopping centers often host summer music concerts—this is a great way for your child to experience a variety of music styles.
- Farmer's markets often pair with music groups to provide musical enjoyment for their customers.
- Many cities enjoy musicals at their "Theatre in the Park" events.
- Sporting events provide fun musical experiences such as live halftime performances, the National Anthem, and special songs played in response to certain happenings during the game.
- Note the music that is playing in stores as you shop or in the elevator as you travel from one floor to another.
- Look for parent-child music classes in your area.
- Attend a high school musical near your home.
- Visit a restaurant that has a mariachi band or a piano player.
- Stop and enjoy the music of street performers.

Magical musical memories and new traditions may be a lasting result of your efforts.

NAPKIN

see Mealtime Bonus Signs (page 164)

NIBBLE

see EAT (page 73)

NIGHT-NIGHT

Place wrist of *cupped hand* palm down on top of other wrist and repeat.

Child may tap arm or back of hand with *open hand*.

♪ Tips for teaching the sign for NIGHT-NIGHT

○ Performing the sign is in itself a confirmation for your child that each time she "signs off" to you with her NIGHT-NIGHT farewell and goes to sleep by herself, she can be certain the sun will rise and you will be there to greet her when she wakes up.

○ When you sign NIGHT-NIGHT, tap your wrist one time for each syllable in NIGHT-NIGHT. Preschool teachers call this phonological awareness. It helps a child understand that words are made of syllables; each syllable in "night-night" gets its own motion. This is a great building block for teaching your child to read.

○ Refer to teaching tips given for BED (page 34) and "Sign Solutions" (page 99, 115, and 142) for more ideas and information about NIGHT-NIGHT.

♪ Songs to sing and sign NIGHT-NIGHT

7. Mister Moon (page 204)
8. We're Having a Bath (page 208)
9. White Sheep and Black Sheep (page 212)
11. Rainbows, Railroads, and Rhymes (page 220)

SIGN SOLUTIONS:
SLEEPING THROUGH THE NIGHT

Q: *My son is eight months old now. He was sleeping for seven or eight hours at a time, but now he is waking up in the night and then staying awake until morning. I am really tired. Could sign language help us get him back into his old sleep routine?*

There is no need for an overnight feeding beyond six months of age. However, periodic arousals occur, more frequently in the first half of the nighttime sleeping hours. Babies need to be able to self-soothe through these periods of arousal and return to sleep on their own. Fifty percent of babies have sleep onset or self-soothing problems at twelve months of age. Developing motor skills such as being able to roll over and pull up can keep babies from lying down and going to sleep. Separation anxiety can also interfere.

Babies will associate certain conditions with falling asleep, and if the conditions change, the baby will not be able to fall asleep. If the condition is always being in mom's arms, mom will have to be there every bedtime *and* at every waking period. This is why it is so important to put the baby in the crib while he is drowsy but not asleep. It is also important to establish a bedtime routine, and put the child to bed at the same time every night. Engage in only quiet activities for thirty minutes before bedtime. Singing, signing, reading, and snuggling are wonderful transition activities prior to putting your child into his crib. Utilize the lullabies on the *Mealtime and Bedtime Sing & Sign* CD as part of your bedtime ritual to keep your child company as he falls asleep.

Transition objects for naps and bedtime are really helpful. Most pediatricians would recommend having a comforting blanket or toy that is always with the child during the bedtime routine and then goes into the crib with the baby. The baby associates this with falling asleep, and if waking occurs in the night, the object is there in the crib with the baby. The baby then has no need to notify the entire household. Giving that transition object a signed name makes it possible for the child to request the treasured item in advance of bedtime.

NOODLES OR MACARONI

Outline the shape of macaroni with both pointer fingers and thumbs in front of chest and continue as you pull fingers away from each other.

Child may open and close fingertips or wiggle pointer fingers on both hands.

♪ Tips for teaching the sign for NOODLES/MACARONI

○ Fill a dish with pasta for you and your child, and dig in with your fingers. Talk and sign MACARONI all the way from your BOWL (page 165) to your mouth. NOODLES are also great food for practicing your spoon skills. Give your toddler a child-size spoon and help him fill it with noodles and direct it to his lips. Praise his spoon technique and efforts. Tell him: "You are eating your NOODLES with a SPOON (page 168). Way to go, buddy."

○ Look at all the shapes, colors, and sizes of pasta at the grocery store on your next shopping trip. Let your child hold a package and take a close look at its contents. Offer your child the chance to choose a package of noodles to buy at the STORE (page 150). Cook up "his NOODLES" for lunch at your earliest convenience.

♪ Song to sing and sign NOODLES/MACARONI

6. What Did You Have for Your Supper? (page 200)

ORANGE

Place *closed fist* at chin, and open and close as if "squeezing" a juicy orange.

Child may place or tap fist on chin.

♪ Tips for teaching the sign for ORANGE

○ The process of learning to speak involves your child's coordination of lips, tongue, and teeth to shape the sounds necessary. Cut an orange section into small bites for both of you to eat. Show her how to "squeeze" the orange with her lips to enjoy its juiciness. Describe "squeezing" the orange again with her teeth by biting the fruit, and "squeezing" it with her tongue by pressing it against the fruit. Sign ORANGE and sustain your squeezing fist action as you tell her to "squeeeeeeeze" her orange with her mouth.

○ The sign for ORANGE is the same for the color as well as the fruit. For a complete set of activities and signs for teaching colors, refer to my *Toddler Sing & Sign* book (see "References and Resources," page 271). Pediatric dietitians suggest feeding toddlers a "rainbow" of fruits and vegetables every day:

> Red—apples, cherries, strawberries, watermelon, red potatoes, tomatoes
> Orange—oranges, peaches, sweet potatoes, carrots
> Yellow—bananas, summer squash, wax beans, pears
> Green—avocados (yes, they're a fruit!), green beans, zucchini, mangos, papayas
> Blue—blueberries
> Purple—grapes, eggplants

(Reprinted with permission from www.wholesometoddlerfood.com; see "References and Resources," page 271.)

○ Some babies are allergic to citrus fruits, so it is recommended that you postpone feeding your child oranges until after her first birthday.

♪ Song to sing and sign ORANGE

4. Fill the Basket (page 192)

♪ Play, Sign, and Learn: ORANGE

Orange Fruit Yogurt

Ingredients:
- 1 small can of mandarin orange slices—drained
- 1 cup plain or vanilla yogurt

Materials:
- Spoon
- Placemat
- Small plastic bowl
- Bib

It's never too early to start cooking with your child. Many a happy memory is made in the kitchen. Orange Fruit Yogurt can be made with the assistance of your youngest and most novice sous chef. Seat your daughter in her chair with a tray or placemat in front of her. Help her put on her bib and prepare to have some fun.

First, open the can of mandarin oranges and give a couple of slices to her. Let her explore, touch, and taste the mandarin orange. Sign and say ORANGE as she explores her new food. "An ORANGE is a FRUIT (page 80). We are going to mix it in our YOGURT (page 169)." It will be fun for your little one to see and feel how the orange changes from one solid piece to many little pieces as she squeezes it in her fingers.

Next, scoop the yogurt into a bowl and add all the oranges, including those prepared by your little assistant. Let her use her fingers to mix the two ingredients, and then help you use the spoon to stir. Encourage her to taste your culinary creation. Tell her, "You are eating our ORANGE FRUIT YOGURT" as she takes a bite. Don't worry if she doesn't seem to like the texture at first. The process of making the yogurt is a fun learning experience. Try it again in a few days. Before long, she will be scooping up her new Orange Fruit Yogurt and eating it ALL-GONE (page 23)!

PACIFIER

see Bedtime Bonus Signs (page 170)

PAJAMAS

Fingers of *open hands*
brush down, up,
and back down on chest

Child may brush hands
on chest several times.

♪ Tips for teaching the sign for PAJAMAS

○ Assemble two or three pajama outfits for your child to choose from: "Do you want your red PAJAMAS or your blue PAJAMAS? Your Bob the Builder PAJAMAS or your Wiggles PAJAMAS?" Giving children ownership of many small choices en route to bedtime makes them more inclined to cooperate with the decision you as a parent make: it is now time to go to SLEEP (page 34).

○ The sign for PAJAMAS seems to recommend that when the child brushes his fingertips on his pajama top, there is something comforting to feel. Some children are calmed or alerted by the type of fabric they wear to bed. Be sensitive to these "touch" preferences. If the silky pajamas tend to wind your child up right before bedtime, perhaps another fabric choice would be best. If your child dons his Superman pj's and spends the next hour trying to run through the house at the speed of light, perhaps that sleep outfit is best to wear while playing in the backyard in the morning. Also consider your child's temperature as they sleep. Some children seem to heat up as they sleep and are sensitive to pajamas that are overly warm. If your child is too warm, it will be more difficult for him to fall asleep.

♪ Song to sing and sign PAJAMAS

10. What'll We Do with the Baby? (page 215)

PANTS

Open hands move upward   Child may touch
on thighs of pants.   or grab pants.

♪ Tips for teaching the sign for PANTS

○ PANTS is a great sign for children to master in anticipation of potty training. To sit on the toilet, they need to know which item of their clothing goes UP (page 156) and DOWN (page 68). You can also discreetly discuss WET (page 172) or DIRTY (page 171) PANTS with your toddler as you begin your toilet teaching. Be sure to purchase pants that are fairly easy for your child to "operate" as she is learning this new skill.

○ Let your child pick the pants she will wear and you can find a shirt that matches, or vice versa. Tell her: "find your PANTS and then we will choose a SHIRT (page 137)."

○ Purchase some clothes for your child's favorite stuffed animal, and let her dress and undress him. Sign PANTS as you put them on and take them off Mr. BEAR (page 32).

♪ Song to sing and sign PANTS

8. We're Having a Bath (page 208)

PARK

see Lullaby Bonus Signs (page 173)

PEACH

Open hand on cheek moves to *gathered fingertips* and away from cheek.

Child may brush cheek with fingertips.

♪ Tips for teaching the sign for PEACH

○ Let your baby choose between strained PEACH or PEAR (page 122). Watch his gaze as you show him a peach and a pear at the fruit market, or jars of peach and pear baby food at the grocery store. Which one does he look at? Treat this subtle "sign" as communication, and tell your child: "I see you looking at the PEACH. I think you want the PEACH today. Then that's what you shall have!"

○ The sign for PEACH is derived from the soft, fuzzy texture of its surface, similar to the soft skin on a person's cheek. Show your child an actual peach and let her touch the skin. Talk about how the skin is soft, just like your child's skin. Touch the peach and then touch your child's cheek. This will reinforce your sign teaching as well, because this helps him feel where the sign "goes" on his face.

♪ Songs to sing and sign PEACH

3. The Muffin Man (page 188)
4. Fill the Basket (page 192)
6. What Did You Have for Your Supper? (page 200)

PEAR

Open hand wraps around
pointer of other hand
and then slides off
to *gathered fingertips.*

Child may grab at one
hand with the other.

♪ Tips for teaching the sign for PEAR

○ You can purchase canned pears and canned PEACHES (page 121) in 100% juice rather than syrup. This is a healthy option for young eaters. Make a pear BOAT (page 170) with canned pear halves positioned with the center facing up on the plate. Fill the "boat" with cottage cheese, add one hungry toddler, and you are "good to go" at snack or mealtime: "Your PEAR is FULL (page 166) of CHEESE (page 55)—YUMMY! (page 86)!"

○ Canned pears cut in bite-sized pieces are wonderful for the new FORK (page 166) user. They are easy to stab and stay on the fork. Pear slices are also a good size and fun texture for self-feeding finger food.

○ For the toddler starting to drink from a straw, make a pear smoothie with canned pears, nonfat vanilla YOGURT (page 169), and MILK (page 102).

♪ Songs to sing and sign PEAR

3. The Muffin Man (page 188)
4. Fill the Basket (page 192)
6. What Did You Have for Your Supper? (page 200)

PEAS

Bent pointer finger taps across the pointer finger of other hand as if touching each pea in a pod.

Child may tap pointer finger on other hand or tap both pointer fingers together.

♪ Tips for teaching the sign for PEAS

○ Peas are a great source of protein, calcium, and vitamins, and can typically be introduced to babies at around six months of age. Peas are wonderful finger foods for babies and toddlers as well as great practice for their developing finger dexterity. You can show him the PEAS sign for each little pea he gobbles!

○ Put one lone pea on a SPOON (page 168) and tell your child: "Here comes your LITTLE (page 166) bite of PEAS!" Ask him: "Do you want MORE (page 107) PEAS? Then load up your spoon with several peas and tell him: "Here comes your BIG (page 164) bite of PEAS!" Ask him what kind of bite he would like next: BIG or LITTLE?

♪ Song to sing and sign PEAS

4. Fill the Basket (page 192)

PIE

see Mealtime Bonus Signs (page 164)

PIG

Place *closed hand* under
chin and move fingers
up and down.

Child may place hand
on or under chin with
or without motion.

♪ Tips for teaching the sign for PIG

○ Read about pigs in picture books, visit one at the zoo or petting farm, or watch them on a farm DVD or television program. Talk with your child about the pig's love for getting DIRTY (page 165) and EATING (page 73) CORN (page 58), and his curly little piggy tail.

○ Play "This Little Piggie" with your child's five toes. Here are the words and actions modified slightly to include sign language practice:

> This little PIGGIE went to market (STORE, page 150),
> This little PIGGIE stayed HOME (page 92),
> This little PIGGIE had roast beef (MEAT, page 101),
> This little PIGGIE had none (ALL-GONE, page 164),
> And this little PIGGIE cried "Wee, wee, wee, all the way HOME!

Tickle or touch a toe—starting with her big toe—at the end of each phrase. Baby will be delighted with your toe touches and focused on your face and hands to see what you will do next: an ideal situation for teaching new signs or practicing familiar ones.

♪ Song to sing and sign PIG

1. My Kitchen Door (page 182)

♪ Play, Sign, and Learn: PIG

Piggy Bank Box

Materials
- Empty tissue box with plastic removed from opening
- Solid-colored paper
- Black permanent marker
- Glue or tape
- 5 or 6 small plastic lids from yogurt containers (in a variety of colors)

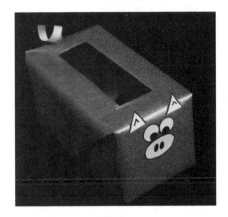

Toddlers love to put things in and take things out. The Piggy Bank Box is a fun organized way for your toddler to exercise this natural exploration. Cover an empty tissue box with solid-colored paper, leaving the tissue hole open. An easy way to do this is to cover the tissue box by placing the tissue hole side of the box on the center of the paper and sealing the paper on the bottom of the box. Next, cut a line lengthwise down the center of the paper covering the oval hole. Then make two cuts sideways from this line just to the depth of the hole. Fold the pieces under the edge of the hole and glue or tape in place. Next, make two small triangles for ears and glue them on the edge of the box. Use your marker to draw two eyes and a pig snout on this end of the box and a curly tail on the other.

Give your child the plastic lid "money" to place in her piggy bank. Say, "Let's put your money in the PIGGY bank" as you sign PIG. Count the "money" as your child places the lids in the bank or talk about the colors of the "coins" as she drops them in the bank. When all the "money" is in the bank, state that "the PIG is FULL (page 166). Let's take the money out." Turn the box over to shake out the coins. Your child will enjoy this game and want to repeat it over and over.

All homemade toys require adult supervision and need to be routinely checked to be sure they are safe. The materials for the Piggy Bank Box could pose a choking hazard if swallowed.

PIRATE

see Lullaby Bonus Signs (page 173)

PLANE

see Lullaby Bonus Signs (page 173)

PLATE

see Mealtime Bonus Signs (page 164)

PLAY OR TOY

Extend thumb and little fingers
of both *closed fists* and twist
both at wrists.

Child may shake both *open
hands* repeatedly.

♪ Tips for teaching the sign for PLAY/TOY

○ A baby learns to solve problems, move, imagine, and respond to his environment through play. Babies need a variety of play activities and opportunities, such as playing alone as well as with others; playing actively as well as quietly; and playing in ways that require concrete as well as imaginative thinking. Remember that play skills—as well as language skills—are mastered through interaction with caring adults. Every minute you spend interacting with your child on the floor with blocks or in the backyard in the sandbox is time well spent.

○ Your child needs to be able to request PLAY from you and will likely select you as the perfect playmate during the first years of his life. Savor this special time in your relationship.

○ Babies and toddlers do not require loads of store-bought toys for play. In fact, it is recommended that you make available a limited number of toys at a time and swap them out occasionally to keep your child excited about his toy options. Give him toy choices: "Do you want this TOY or that TOY?" and model all the possible ways to play with a toy so that your child can imitate your actions and then learn to initiate them on his own.

 Songs to sing and sign PLAY/TOY

PLEASE

Rub *open hand* on upper chest in circular motion.

Child may place hand on chest without circular motion, or pat chest.

Tips for teaching the sign for PLEASE

○ Just as you remind your child to say "please" when she wants something, help her sign PLEASE in the same context. This is an easy sign to master because your child already wants something from you—a snack, a hug, a toy—and will quickly catch on that her gesture will make you smile and promptly deliver "the goods." In fact, PLEASE is one of the best signs to help children grasp the relationship between their hand movements and getting what they want. They learn that you will consistently provide their desired object or action if they rub their chest, and realize that perhaps your other hand motions mean something as well.

○ Enlist the help of other caring adults and siblings in using the PLEASE sign to speak and sign to you. Signing with others becomes the "training video" for your child as she figures out how communication works: each person takes a turn, you look at and listen to one another, you are making interesting faces as you make your sounds and signs.

○ Toddlers often substitute PLEASE for MORE as they grow. Many parents teach their children to combine PLEASE with other signs, for example: MORE (page 107) PLEASE, MILK (page 102) PLEASE, and DOWN (page 68) PLEASE (from the high chair or crib).

♪ Songs to sing and sign PLEASE

1. My Kitchen Door (page 182)
3. The Muffin Man (page 188)
4. Fill the Basket (page 192)
7. Mister Moon (page 204)

SIGN OF SUCCESS

"I am a parent educator. While working with the children I served this week, I was thrilled to see many of them using the sign for PLEASE. Each time I said the word 'please' I also circled my chest with my open hand. A two-year-old child walked up to me, handed me his cup, and made continual circular motions near his tummy. A one-year-old child patted her chest while she sat in her high chair waiting for her snack. What well-mannered children we all have!"

–Kelly H.

POTATO

Two curved *open fingers* tap
top of other fist multiple times.

Child may tap fist with one
finger, fist, or *open hand*.

♪ Tips for teaching the sign for POTATO

○ POTATO is an easy sign for your child to perform. It may look like the sign for GRAPE (page 88); however, you know your child best and will sense from the context which food they are most likely requesting.

○ Decorate mashed potatoes with CORN (page 58) niblets. Let baby explore his food by placing corn niblets on the mashed potatoes and pushing them down into the potatoes. Then help baby use his spoon to search for the corn. Help him scoop up the mashed potatoes with his SPOON (page 168) and take a bite as you ask, "Any CORN in that bite? No? Let's try some MORE (page 107)!" You can also HIDE (page 91) cooked PEAS (page 123) or diced CARROTS (page 49).

♪ Songs to sing and sign POTATO

5. John the Rabbit (page 195)
10. What'll We Do with the Baby? (page 215)

For a wonderful sweet potato pancake recipe, visit: http://www.wholesomebabyfood
.com/pastariceforbaby.htm.

♪ Play, Sign, and Learn: POTATO

Mr. Potato Head

Materials
- Large baking potato
- Canned carrot slices
- Pieces of cheese
- Shredded carrots
- Grape or cherry tomatoes
- Placemat
- Bib

"Mr. Potato Head" toys have been popular for generations. Children can spend hours creatively designing face after face on their potato head canvas. Adults are also eager to join in the fun and demonstrate their creative talents. Young and old alike will delight in taking their potato head skills to another level by using real potatoes and other edible accessories.

Cut the potatoes in thirds by cutting lengthwise from end to end. Eat or discard the center piece. Use the "faces" of the potato for decorating—one for you and one for your child. Invite your child to come play "Mr. Potato Head" with you. Hand him the potato head and say: "We are going to make a face on our POTATOES. Let's put eyes on our POTATOES first." Model each step of the creation process for your child by placing the "body parts" on your potato, and then have him imitate you by placing the food items on his potato. First, add canned carrot slices for the eyes. Next, use a piece of cheese for the nose and add a quarter of a grape tomato as the mouth. Top your potato head with shredded carrot hair. Admire your creations and label all of the parts.

- You can place a small mirror on the table for you and your child to look at your own facial features as you place the items on your potatoes
- Put a toy potato head on the table as a model.
- For creative inspiration, read *How Are You Peeling? Foods with Moods* by Saxton Freymann and Joost Elffers (see "Sing and Sign—and Read—with Picture Books," page 247).
- Think of other food items that you can use to decorate your potatoes, such as shredded cheese hair, green bean eyebrows, and mushroom ears.

The small pieces of raw vegetables used in this activity require adult supervision as they could pose a choking hazard if swallowed.

POUR

see Mealtime Bonus Signs (page 164)

PRAY

Bring *closed hands* together under chin.

Child may bring *closed hands* together or may clasp fingers together.

♪ Tips for teaching the sign for PRAY

○ Until she is able to speak for herself, signing makes it possible for a child to begin expressing gratitude for the things she cares about. Watch your child to see her anticipate your mealtime or bedtime prayers by clasping her hands under her chin if prayer is part of your routine.

○ Your mealtime prayer or blessing can simply be a THANK YOU (page 168) to God for FOOD (page 73). Include a simple prayer in your nighttime routine that gives your child the chance to say THANK YOU to God for FOOD and TOYS (page 126) and each of the people and pets she loves. However, leave your child's prayers open-ended so that she can add things or people she is grateful for.

○ Create a place for your nighttime prayers. It can be with your child leaning against your chest in the rocking chair; you can reach around her body to help her form the PRAY sign with your hands on hers. Perhaps that special place will be in your arms as you bow your foreheads onto one another's and pray before you put her in her crib or bed. You can also show her how to kneel with you next to her bed.

♪ Songs to sing and sign PRAY

PUDDING

see Mealtime Bonus Signs (page 164)

PUMPKIN

see Mealtime Bonus Signs (page 164)

RABBIT

Bend *closed hands* at top of head to form "bunny ears."

Child may touch hands or fingertips to sides or top of head.

♪ Tips for teaching the sign for RABBIT

○ Babies and toddlers love the RABBIT's long, floppy ears and the sign is an easy one to teach for that reason: your child will form rabbit ears with his hands on top of his head. It is also an easy sign to spot because few "baby signs" require your child to touch the top of his head with both hands.

○ Watch the way rabbits twitch their noses and hop. Ask your child to move his nose like a rabbit. Show him a mirror and demonstrate by twitching your nose with enthusiasm. Bounce your "baby bunny" in your lap as you say: "You are my BUNNY! Look at you hop!" Help your toddler hop like a rabbit by taking his hands in yours and lifting him off the ground as you say: "hop, hop, hop!"

○ Make a tricky rabbit TOY (page 126) by tying rope, yarn, or twine to a stuffed rabbit and lifting up and down to help him "hop." Let your child make the bunny hop with your supervision.

♪ Song to sing and sign RABBIT

5. John the Rabbit (page 195)

RAILROAD

see Lullaby Bonus Signs (page 173)

RAINBOW

see Lullaby Bonus Signs (page 173)

READ

see Lullaby Bonus Signs (page 173)

RESTAURANT

see Mealtime Bonus Signs (page 164)

ROCK (IN A ROCKING CHAIR)

see Bedtime Bonus Signs (page 170)

ROLLER COASTER

see Lullaby Bonus Signs (page 173)

ROOM

see Bedtime Bonus Signs (page 170)

ROOSTER

Make a rooster's "comb"
with thumb and curved
pointer and middle fingers,
and tap forehead.

Child may place her
thumb or hand on
her cheek, brow,
or another head location.

♪ Tips for teaching the sign for ROOSTER

○ Put on some music and do a fancy rooster strut as you sign ROOSTER and sing: "Cock-a-doodle-doo!" As she does with other animals, your child may call this animal a "cock-a-doodle-doo" instead of a "rooster" as she signs ROOSTER.

○ Borrow the tune to "Here We Go 'Round the Mulberry Bush" and sing a verse that goes like this: "This is the way the ROOSTER struts . . ." Clap your hands to the chorus: "Here we go round my baby's FARM (page 173)!"

○ Add rice, sand, beans, or popcorn kernels to some plastic Easter eggs. Using a glue gun, fasten the two halves of the egg together securely, and cover the seam with plastic tape. Let your little rooster shake his tail feathers and his musical egg at the same time!

♪ Song to sing and sign ROOSTER

10. What'll We Do with the Baby? (page 215)

SANDWICH

see Mealtime Bonus Signs (page 164)

SCARED

see Bedtime Bonus Signs (page 170)

SEA

see Lullaby Bonus Signs (page 173)

SHAMPOO

see Bedtime Bonus Signs (page 170)

SHEEP

Make cutting motions as if "shearing the sheep" with *two open fingers* on top of other arm. Move the "shears" up the extended arm.	Child may pat or place fingertips or hand on extended arm.

♪ Tips for teaching the sign for SHEEP

○ Visit your county fair, 4-H event, or petting zoo so your child can feel the sheep's wooly coat. Many pet sheep I have met are cooperative about having little hands on their tummies and backs as long as the children are gentle (and the child is supervised by an adult). Once your child has seen—and touched—a real sheep, he will be more likely to remember the sign for SHEEP than had he simply looked at a picture of one in a book.

○ Sing and sign "Baa Baa Black SHEEP" and teach your child to answer: "Yes, sir, yes, sir, three bags FULL!" with her sign for FULL (page 166). Sing and sign, "Mary Had a Little LAMB" and substitute your child's name for Mary's.

○ Children love to make the "baa" sound of the lamb. Join your child in a sheep game: get on all fours side by side in your living room "pasture" and "baa" until the cows come home!

♪ Song to sing and sign SHEEP

9. White Sheep and Black Sheep (page 212)

SIGN OF SUCCESS

"I read my daughter the book *Brown Bear, Brown Bear, What Do You See?* (see "Sing and Sign—and Read—with Picture Books," page 247). There's a page that talks about a 'black sheep.' I signed and sang the entire book to the tune of 'Twinkle, Twinkle Little Star.' I could tell from my daughter's attention to the book that associating music, signs, and picture books was a great way to teach new signs."

—Myra V.

SHIRT

Thumb and pointer finger
pinch and lift shirt at shoulder.

Child may grab
or point to shirt.

♪ Tips for teaching the sign for SHIRT

○ Ask your child to HELP (page 90) you sort the clean clothes in the laundry basket before you fold them. Ask her to find all her SHIRTS. Can she find her PANTS (page 120) and SOCKS (page 144) as well? Perhaps you could find her a small laundry basket all her own to put her clean clothes into as you sort.

○ Look at photographs of family members and point to their shirts. Combine your sign words as you describe what you see in the pictures: DADDY (page 61) SHIRT, MOMMY (page 104) SHIRT, GRANDMA (page 174) SHIRT. You can also help your child describe and choose her shirts using sign language according to the picture they have on the front: "Do you want your DOGGIE (page 67) SHIRT or your BUTTERFLY (page 48) SHIRT?"

○ Talk about shirts that are big and little. Put DADDY's or GRANDPA's (page 174) BIG (page 164) SHIRT on your child. Let her crawl or walk in the big shirt. Let daddy or grandpa try and put on your child's shirt. Make sure they make their attempt into a comedy routine for your child. Sign BIG and LITTLE (page 166) SHIRT as you give your child one of her first lessons in comparing and contrasting two things.

♪ Song to sing and sign SHIRT

8. We're Having a Bath (page 208)

SHOES

Tap thumb side of fists
together two times.

Child may tap fists
together once or
several times. Child may
also point to shoe.

♪ Tips for teaching the sign for SHOES

○ Describe your shoes with sign language: WATER (page 161) SHOES for going swimming; PLAY (page 126) SHOES for playing outside; BED (page 34) SHOES you wear with your PAJAMAS (page 119). "We are going to the swimming pool. What SHOES do we need?"

○ Make a game of sorting shoes. Put several pairs in the middle of your room, including big shoes from your closet as well. Let your child sort the shoes. MOMMY's (page 104) SHOES in her closet, DADDY'S (page 61) SHOES for mowing the yard in the garage, BABY'S (page 27) SHOES on the shelf in his room. Baby loves the satisfaction of being "big" and helping you by being your shoe sorter.

♪ Song to sing and sign SHOES

8. We're Having a Bath (page 208)

♪ Play, Sign, and Learn: SHOE

Shoes Galore!

> *"One shoe off and one shoe on.*
> *Diddle diddle dumpling, my son John!"*
> —DIDDLE DIDDLE DUMPLING
> (ORIGIN UNKNOWN)

Shoes are enchanting to children. To a little one, nothing is better than a shoe, whether they have buckles or laces, are made of leather or cloth, are white or blue! Children are intrigued by shoes of all sizes: daddy's shoes, mommy's shoes, baby's shoes. Shoes are fun. So fun that they remain a hit with adults as well. Few can resist a good pair of shoes.

For toddlers and babies, shoes can be a tremendous source of fun and learning. Many concepts can be taught through experiences and play with shoes:

- Line them up. Help your child make a line or train of shoes. Talk about how you want to organize them—side by side with toes in front? Toe to heel? "I like your SHOE TRAIN (page 175). Choo-choo, I see the SHOES!"
- Play "Go Fish." Start by collecting seven to nine pairs of shoes (any odd number). Separate the shoes into two piles: one for you and one for your child. Keep some of the pairs together and sort some of the pairs into the two piles. Now you are ready to play. First, help your child find the matching pairs in her pile. Have her help you find the matching pairs in your pile. Put the matching pairs aside in a "collective winning area." If you find all the matching pairs of shoes, the two of you will win! Next, ask your child, "Do you have this SHOE?" Hold up a shoe and let your child search for the match in her pile. Help her be successful in her search. When she finds the match, act excited and put these shoes with the other matching sets. Continue playing until you have found all the matching shoes. When searching for a match, describe the shoes with a word: blue or red, buckle or laces, big or little? This is a great way to expose your child to a variety of new adjectives.

- Make your own shoes. Decorate two rectangular, empty tissue boxes using paint, markers, or stickers. Remove the plastic insert in the opening of each box and use hot glue or Superglue to adhere a nonslip bath appliqué to the bottom of each tissue box. Once the glue is dry, assist your child in putting on the homemade shoes by slipping the tissue boxes over the shoes he is wearing. Hold his hands and help him walk around the room.

All homemade toys require adult supervision and need to be routinely checked to be sure they are safe. Also, monitor for safety when your child is trying on shoes that are too big.

SING

see MUSIC (page 111)

SISTER

see Lullaby Bonus Signs (page 173)

SIT

see CHAIR (page 54)

SLEEP

see BED (page 34)

SMELL

see Mealtime Bonus Signs (page 164)

SMILE

Pointer fingers draw a smile from the corners of the mouth as one smiles.

Child may point to smile.

♪ Tips for teaching the sign for SMILE

○ What does it mean when DADDY (page 61) crinkles his eyes and stretches his lips from side to side? Baby learns that SMILE and HAPPY (page 89) and that weird crinkly-eyed, lip-stretching look on Dad's face all go together. After she figures out this relationship, she will do her best to make him smile by imitating the same facial expression. She may also put her hands on Daddy's cheeks and try to push or stretch them into the smiling position. Either strategy works on most of the daddies I know!

○ As you wait during appointments; as you cruise your baby in the grocery cart, car seat, or stroller; or while you wait for your food at a restaurant, redirect potential "I'm tired of waiting" meltdowns by encouraging your child to look at people with smiling faces. "Look at the HAPPY GIRL (page 83)! She is SMILING."

○ Refer to teaching tips given for HAPPY for more ideas.

♪ Song to sing and sign SMILE

9. White Sheep and Black Sheep (page 212)

SNUGGLE

see LOVE (page 98)

SIGN SOLUTIONS: SMOOTH TRANSITIONS

Q: *My daughter pitches a fit when it is time to transition from one activity to another, such as from leaving somewhere she likes to go to the car or from mealtime to go to a nap. She has a sign vocabulary of twenty words she uses to communicate with me. Can I channel her signed communication skills to make transitions easier for her?*

Using the ALL-DONE (page 23) sign has been particularly useful for parents in assisting children as they move from one motivating and desirable activity to something less so. Use ALL-DONE or STOP (page 149) to communicate to your child that it is time to leave grandma's house, the park, or McDonald's Play Place and head for home or another destination. Then redirect your child with a song or a tickle as you travel. Using signed and spoken words to explain to your child what other activities are in store that day will also help ease the transition as well.

SOAP

Fingers of one *closed hand* brush the palm of other *closed hand two times.*

Child may rub hands together as if washing them or rub one hand on the palm of other several times.

♪ Tips for teaching the sign for SOAP

○ Help teach your child that soap helps us get clean when we are DIRTY (page 165). We wash DIRTY PANTS (page 120) in the washing machine, DIRTY hands before we EAT (page 73), DOGGIE's (page 67) DIRTY paws after he walks through the mud in the yard. Get him in the habit of using soap to WASH (page 31) hands before mealtime.

○ Add soap and teach him how to wash his hands properly by rubbing his palms, the tops of his hands and in between his fingers. Ask your child to use plenty of SOAP or to pass you the SOAP. Show him how to turn over his hands under the water. You can compose a little hand washing ditty to make SOAPY hands fun!

♪ Songs to sing and sign SOAP

8. We're Having a Bath (page 208)
10. What'll We Do with the Baby? (page 215)

SIGN OF SUCCESS

"My daughter likes to show me where all the things necessary for bathtime are, so we made that part of our routine. She HELPS me locate our essential items: SOAP, SHAMPOO (page 172), CUP (page 165), and BOAT (page 170). They are all stored in a predictable location in the bathroom in a plastic bucket, so 'helping me' is easy for her."

—Gwen L.

SOCKS

Pointer fingers rub against each other while pointing away from body.

Child may tap one pointer finger against the other. Child may also point to sock.

♪ Tips for teaching the sign for SOCKS

○ Load up a laundry basket with clean socks from your closet and HIDE (page 91) your baby under the sock pile: "Where is my baby? Oh my, she is HIDING in my SOCKS!" Show her how to hide small TOYS (page 126) or stuffed animals under the sock pile. Hide one sock under a burp cloth or baby BLANKET (page 37). Take the cloth off with a flourish to reveal the sock underneath. This is guaranteed to make your baby giggle!

○ Let your baby dump a basket of socks on the floor and show her how to match the pairs. She can hand them to you when she has finished HELPING (page 90) you match each pair. Show your appreciation by saying THANK YOU (page 168) for helping you.

○ Roll your socks into a ball and throw them into a laundry basket. This is great target practice for your child's developing eye-hand coordination. Put socks on your hands and make them into impromptu puppets. No button eyes or nose are necessary; just a sense of humor and imagination.

♪ Song to sing and sign SOCKS

8. We're Having a Bath (page 208)

SONG

see MUSIC (page 111)

SPAGHETTI

see Mealtime Bonus Signs (page 164)

SPIDER

see Lullaby Bonus Signs (page 173)

SPLASH

Closed hands with palms down alternately "splash" as if playing in imaginary water.

Child may use open hands to pretend to splash water.

♪ Tips for teaching the sign for SPLASH

○ Splashing is fun! One of the first purposeful movements your baby can perform is lifting his arms up and down. When doing this motion in the bathtub, his effort is rewarded with a good self-splashing. He will inevitably look baffled as if he blames you for being the "splasher." After he figures out that he is the one doing the splashing, he will love repeating his trick again and again.

○ Children drip dry, so don't be afraid to get them damp to teach them the sign for SPLASH. Supervise them as they splash while putting their hand on the stream of water from the garden hose or sprinkler. Give them a bucket of WATER (page 161) to play with on your driveway, and some CUPS (page 165) or scoops for pouring water. Show them how to scoop the water and throw it to splash the driveway. Watch as the water falls DOWN (page 68)!

O Refer to teaching tips given for WATER for more ideas.

♪ Song to sing and sign SPLASH

10. What'll We Do with the Baby? (page 215)

SPOON

see Mealtime Bonus Signs (page 164)

STAR

Pointer fingers rub against each other as they are lifted "in the sky."

Child may lift hands and wiggle fingers over head or tap pointer fingers together.

♪ Tips for teaching the sign for STAR

O Young children master two separate meanings for "star": the bright light in the nighttime sky and the shape they will learn to recognize in preschool. Incorporate both in your play-based teaching of the sign for STAR.

O Use a star cookie cutter to shape a CHEESE (page 55) or APPLE (page 25) slice for your child. Purchase a star-shaped sponge or create one with scissors and a kitchen sponge;

help your child use the sponge to dip in tempera paint and blot on paper. You can also try painting with ORANGE (page 117), lemon, or lime halves, or by carving the shape of a star in a POTATO (page 129).

♪ Song to sing and sign STAR

12. Now I Lay Me Down to Sleep (page 224)

SIGN OF SUCCESS

"I first taught this sign as we sat together on our deck at night. I would point to the stars and say and sign STAR, and then take my daughter's hands and help her do the sign. She quickly began to sign STAR on her own when she would see stars in the sky."

—Melissa K.

♪ Play, Sign, and Learn: STAR

Edible Star Art

Materials:
- Gerber Fruit Puffs or Veggie Puffs
- Small bowl
- Yogurt
- Spoon
- Placemat
- Bib

Star light, star bright, how many stars will I eat tonight? There is such satisfaction in the creation of art, especially an edible masterpiece. Your toddler will be excited to create and consume her Edible Star Art. Start by seating your child at the table with her bib and a clean placemat. Tell her that it's time to make a star picture. Next, use a spoon to make a very small dot of yogurt on the placemat. This little dollop of yogurt will serve as your "glue dot." Then select a star-shaped fruit or veggie puff from the small bowl and place it on the yogurt "glue." Notice the position of your fingers as you select the star puff from the bowl. You are holding the star between your thumb and pointer finger. This grasp is called a pincer grasp, and it is an important developmental skill for a baby. It is her first grasp of precision. The process of creating Edible Star Art will provide many opportunities for her to practice this important skill.

Show the bowl of star puffs to your daughter. Let her feel them and explore them with her fingers. Sign and say STAR as she touches the star puffs. Next, make two or three dots of yogurt on the placemat and tell her: "Let's put STARS on the dots." Help her by guiding her hand to the dots and releasing the star on the dot. Praise her for her efforts. Don't be surprised if she wants to eat her star as soon as she is finished putting it on the placemat. This is fine, because Edible Star Art is more about the process than the product. Continue to create your art by adding two or three dots of yogurt at a time. Encourage your daughter to continue placing star puffs on the dots you create. After you have a few in place, tell her: "It's time to eat the STARS." Count the stars as she eats them by saying and signing "one STAR, two STARS," and so on.

Gerber suggests that your baby is ready for Fruit and Veggie Puffs when she is able to eat thick, lumpy foods with large pieces, crawl on her hands and knees, and mash food with her gums to chew.

STIR

see Mealtime Bonus Signs (page 164)

STOP

Move little-finger side of
one closed hand abruptly
onto palm of other hand in a
single chopping motion.

Child may clap one
hand with the other or
place *closed hands* in
front of body.

♪ Tips for teaching the sign for STOP

○ Play a swinging game and sing a song of your own creation including the words swing
and STOP. Ask your child if he would like to swing some MORE (page 107) and prompt
him to sign this word. Then repeat the "Swing and Stop" game until it is your child's idea
to STOP!

○ Stop and go along with your child. You can play a "Freeze" game, where you dance or run
or clap along to the music, and then freeze or STOP when the music stops. Tell your toddler to draw a line or color a picture until you say STOP. Or SPLASH (page 145) water in
the bathtub and STOP. My favorite activity for stop and go play is DANCING (page 62).
Hold him close as you twirl and glide—and then STOP as you tip him backwards!

♪ Songs to sing and sign STOP

4. Fill the Basket (page 192)
9. White Sheep and Black Sheep (page 212)

STORE

Gathered fingertips of both hands rock upward and away from body in front of chest several times.

Child may shake fists in front of chest.

♪ Tips for teaching the sign for STORE

○ Talk about all the different kinds of stores you visit together: grocery, hardware, plant and flower, pet, clothing. Combine signed vocabulary words to describe them: FOOD (page 73) STORE, and FLOWER (page 77) STORE; DOG (page 67) or CAT (page 51) pet STORE. Talk about what you will purchase at each.

○ Make your own store. Save boxes, plastic bottles, and bags from the foods you purchase. Clean them, tape them closed, and add them to your game. (Tin cans are fine to include as long as the inside edges are hammered flat and covered with plastic tape.) You can purchase some plastic fruits and vegetables to include healthy choices and more sign language teaching opportunities at your "store." Find a large plastic box or laundry basket and dedicate it to this play activity. It will be used to store your "groceries" and can be turned upside down to serve as your checkout stand. Have fun shopping, and remember that good customers always ask lots of questions: "Excuse me, STORE GIRL (page 83), what FRUIT (page 80) is this? It looks YUMMY (page 86). THANK YOU (page 168) for your HELP (page 90)!"

♪ Songs to sing and sign STORE

3. The Muffin Man (page 188)
5. John the Rabbit (page 195)

STRAW

see Mealtime Bonus Signs (page 164)

SUN

Cup one hand and touch thumb to eyebrow.

Child may touch fingertips to head or *cupped hand* to brow or cheek.

♪ Tips for teaching the sign for SUN

○ Discuss the sun and how it helps us decide what we wear and what we can we do: "There's the SUN. It will be a warm day so we can go to the park. Those PANTS (page 120) and that SHIRT (page 137) will be plenty warm for today." Teach your child to look out the window and see if the sun is in the sky or HIDING (page 91) behind a cloud.

○ There are many fun folk songs to sing and sign about the sun. One of my favorites is "You Are My Sunshine." Steve Metzger added some perfect verses to his picture book version of this classic song (see "Sing and Sign—and Read—with Picture Books," page 247). Sing and sign his story about "LOVE (page 98) shine" and "STAR (page 146) shine," along with our favorite SUNshine.

♪ Song to sing and sign SUN

7. Mister Moon (page 204)

SUPPER

see EAT (page 73)

SWEET

see Mealtime Bonus Signs (page 164)

SWIM

see Lullaby Bonus Signs (page 173)

TABLE

see Mealtime Bonus Signs (page 164)

TASTE

see Mealtime Bonus Signs (page 164)

THANK YOU

see Mealtime Bonus Signs (page 164)

THIRSTY

see Mealtime Bonus Signs (page 164)

TIME (FOR BED)

see Bedtime Bonus Signs (page 170)

TIRED

see BED (page 34)

TOAST

see Mealtime Bonus Signs (page 164)

TOMATO

Pointer finger touches lips and then slides down gathered fingertips of other hand as if slicing a tomato.

Child may use pointer finger or whole hand in slicing motion against other fist.

♪ Tips for teaching the sign for TOMATO

○ Babies and toddlers love the bright red color and "ball shape" of tomatoes. Grape tomatoes cut in half are great finger food for toddlers.

○ Grow a tomato plant in your backyard or in a container on your patio. Talk about how SUN (page 151) and WATER (page 161) make the TOMATO plant grow. Look at the FLOWERS (page 77) that grow first, followed by LITTLE (page 166) tomatoes, and finally BIG (page 164) tomatoes ready to pick, WASH (page 31), and EAT (page 73). Let your little gardener WATER the tomato plant each day and watch the tomatoes grow.

○ Talk to your child about tomatoes in other dishes, such as tomato sauce with CHEESE (page 55) and NOODLES (page 116) or tomato soup. Prepare a grilled cheese sandwich for your child and cut it into strips or chunks for your child to dip into tomato soup.

♪ Songs to sing and sign TOMATO

4. Fill the Basket (page 192)
5. John the Rabbit (page 195)

TOWEL

see Bedtime Bonus Signs (page 170)

TOY

see PLAY (page 126)

TRACTOR

see Lullaby Bonus Signs (page 173)

TRAIN

see Lullaby Bonus Signs (page 173)

TREE

Place elbow of *open hand*
on top of other hand and
rotate wrist of *open hand.*

Child may hold one or
both hands up in the air.

♪ Tips for teaching the sign for TREE

○ Most babies and toddlers do not fully appreciate the true amazement of trees until we draw attention to them. Point out trees on your outings together. "This TREE has white FLOWERs (page 77). Wow, that TREE is so tall." Plan a fun day at an apple orchard. Talk about the apple trees as you walk through the orchard and let your child choose which tree to pick first.

○ All babies and toddlers love exploring the yard with their grown-ups. Count the TREES as your child runs and touches each one. Hang streamers in your TREES when you have an outdoor party or BBQ. Play "Hide-and-Seek" behind your trees and sing "Ring-around-the-Rosie" as you circle around a tree. Include trees in all of your outside experiences.

♪ Songs to sing and sign TREE

5. John the Rabbit (page 195)
7. Mister Moon (page 204)
9. White Sheep and Black Sheep (page 212)

TUMMY

Touch stomach
with closed hand.

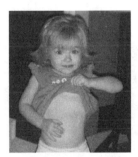
Child may touch stomach
with pointer finger, whole
hand, or both hands.

♪ Tips for teaching the sign for TUMMY

○ Give your baby's tummy lots of kisses and an occasional tickle or buzz by blowing gently on her skin and making a funny sound. Play "Peek-a-Boo" with baby's tummy: cover her stomach with your hands as you say: "WHERE (page 162) is your TUMMY?" and then take your hands away and exclaim: "There's my baby's TUMMY!"

○ If you own an exercise ball, place your child facing down with her tummy on the ball and gently roll her as you sing a tummy rolling song of your own making. The rolling motion shifts the fluid in her inner ear (called vestibular stimulation), which helps children master posture and balance. Children seek out this kind of sensory experience. That is why she loves you to swing and bounce her.

○ WASH (page 31) your child's TUMMY in the bathtub. Wash her rubber DUCK's (page 71) TUMMY or let the child wash your tummy. Point to tummies in picture books. Find tummies on stuffed animals and baby dolls, pets, and parents.

♪ Song to sing and sign TUMMY

3. The Muffin Man (page 188)

TURKEY

see Mealtime Bonus Signs (page 164)

UP

 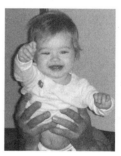

Pointer finger points and moves in upward motion.   Child may point up without movement.

♪ Tips for teaching the sign for UP

○ Say UP as you pick baby up from the floor, her high chair, or crib. You may want to teach your child to sign UP when he requests that you pick him up: "Do you want me to pick you UP? Show me UP. Good talking with your hands!"

○ Show your child things that go up: hot-air balloons, BIRDS (page 36), PLANES (page 174), mountaintops, tall buildings, kites, BUTTERFLIES (page 48), and flying BUGS (page 46). RAINBOWS (page 174), clouds, SUN (page 151), and MOON (page 105) are all up, up, up!

❍ Show your child how to move his body up and DOWN (page 68). Hold his rib cage with your hands and help him jump up and down, or bounce him gently on an exercise ball as he sits on his bottom. Hold him and jump up and down. Bounce a ball up and down. Walk up stairs and say and sign UP with each step.

❍ Refer to teaching tips given for DOWN for more ideas.

♪ Songs to sing and sign UP

3. The Muffin Man (page 188)
7. Mister Moon (page 204)
9. White Sheep and Black Sheep (page 212)

♪ Play, Sign, and Learn: UP

Up and Down Line Art

Materials:
- Easel or space on wall or fridge for large piece of drawing paper
- Large pieces of drawing paper
- Washable markers
- Washable paint and paintbrush
- Slide whistle

Toddlers are constantly experiencing the words up and down. We pick them up and put them down. We tell them to stand up and to sit down. We go up the stairs and back down again. Balloons, airplanes, and birds go up. The food on their high chair tray goes down to the floor. However, toddlers have limited opportunities to make something go both up and down.

For the Up and Down Line Art activity, toddlers will listen to your voice and draw in relation to the concept you say. Place a large piece of drawing paper on an easel or tape it on the wall or refrigerator. Take a washable marker and model for your toddler. Increase the pitch of your voice as you say the word "up." At the same time, starting at the bottom of your paper, use a marker to draw a line that goes up to the top of the page. Sign the word UP each time you say it. Next, say, "down" and lower the pitch of your voice as you lower the marker back down the page. Tell your toddler, "Now, it's your turn to draw UP." Help your toddler hold the marker and gently guide his hand to draw a line up to the top of the page as you say "up" with your high-pitched voice. Next, tell him, "It's time to draw DOWN (page 68)." Gently guide his hand back down the page as you say "down," lowering the pitch of your speaking voice. Change marker colors and repeat. Be silly with your voice as you play with your toddler.

- As your toddler becomes more independent with this game, add excitement by varying the rate at which you say and sign the UP and DOWN. Change your volume, too. Add new pages to the easel and let you toddler create a collection of line drawings.
- Another fun way to explore up and down with this game is by using a slide whistle. Instead of changing the pitch of your voice to match the direction you give, use the slide whistle instead. Say and sign UP and then pull the slide out as you blow the whistle. Next, say DOWN as you push the slide back in the whistle.
- Try painting with washable paint and a paintbrush as you explore the concepts of up and down. Encourage your child to move his body up and down as he paints by going up on his tiptoes as he paints up and bending his knees as he paints down.

VEGETABLE

see Mealtime Bonus Signs (page 164)

WAFFLE

see Mealtime Bonus Signs (page 164)

WAKE

see Bedtime Bonus Signs (page 170)

WALK

Both *closed hands* palm down, alternate moving forward in imitation of feet taking steps.

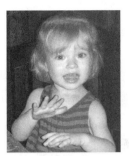

Child may alternate hands up and down without moving forward as if feet are walking in place.

♪ Tips for teaching the sign for WALK

○ Carry your baby as you WALK or load her into the stroller and make a walk part of your daily routine. Tell her stories about all the things you see. She will learn to point and perhaps grunt or vocalize to request a spoken word or sign for each and every item she wants to learn. Walks with your baby will be language-rich opportunities for you to share the world with her.

○ Toddlers like to walk at every opportunity. Make WALKS a part of your daily routine if possible. The sign for WALK then becomes your toddler's way to request a WALK to the park or through the neighborhood with you. Make your expectations clear from the start when it comes to your toddler's safety and walking: "Do you want to hold my left hand or my right hand when you WALK across the street with me? You can WALK or I will carry you, but we can't choose running in the parking lot."

○ Refer to teaching tips for GO (page 85) for more ideas.

♪ Song to sing and sign WALK

9. White Sheep and Black Sheep (page 212)

WANT

Pull open fingers toward
body one time with palms up
and fingertips slightly curved,
as if drawing something
desirable toward you.

Child may open and close
hands several times.

♪ Tips for teaching the sign for WANT

○ After your baby can roll over on her own, he has graduated from the first stage of infancy to a little person with preferences and opinions. Now is the time to begin asking him: "What do you WANT, baby BOY (page 39)? Do you WANT to look out the window at the pretty BIRDIES (page 36)?" Give your child's wishes and whims a voice by labeling them and then responding. Your sensitivity to your child's earliest efforts at communication will enhance the bond between the two of you and help you recognize the subtle— or not so subtle—cues he gives you to get his needs met.

○ Share your own "wants" with your child so he can begin to understand the relationship between our desire and action: "I WANT food because I am HUNGRY (page 93) so I will EAT (page 73) a healthy snack," or "I WANT GRAPES (page 88) so I will buy some at the STORE (page 150) today."

○ Use the WANT sign to help your child when he has a meltdown by expressing his frustration and anger with words. Tell him, "You WANT to stay at your FRIEND's (page 79) house because you are having fun. You don't WANT to GO (page 85) because you like your FRIEND."

♪ Songs to sing and sign WANT

4. Fill the Basket (page 192)
6. What Did You Have for Your Supper? (page 200)

WASH

see BATH (page 31)

WASH-HAIR

see Bedtime Bonus Signs (page 170)

WATER

Extend pointer, middle, and ring fingers of one hand. Place tip of pointer finger at side of mouth and tap.

Child may touch or tap chin with fingers.

♪ Tips for teaching the sign for WATER

○ Make water your child's preferred drink choice and offer it frequently. WATER then becomes a word your child will use to request a drink when she is thirsty. Drinking enough water is critically important for learning, development, and growth.

○ Water, water everywhere: bathtime, hoses, sprinklers, swimming pools, sinks, showers, washing machines, raindrops, fountains, streams, rivers, lakes, oceans, and so on. Show your child the WATER in each location you encounter. Talk about how animals love WATER: DUCKS (page 71) swim in WATER, PIGS (page 124) like to roll in DIRTY (page 171) WATER, your pet DOGGIE (page 67) loves his WATER BOWL (page 165).

○ Although the word WET (page 172) has a different sign, some parents choose to use the sign for WATER to teach their child this concept as well.

○ Give your child a bucket of WATER and a clean, soft paintbrush. Let her dip the brush in water and "paint" the driveway. Let her paint you as well! You can also fill a clean spray bottle with water and show your child how to WASH (page 31) a lawn CHAIR (page 54), a TOY (page 126), or GRANDPA (page 174).

○ Refer to teaching tips given for SPLASH (page 145) for more ideas.

♪ Song to sing and sign WATER

6. What Did You Have for Your Supper? (page 200)

WET

see Bedtime Bonus Signs (page 170)

WHERE

Wave pointer finger back
and forth in the air.

Child may wave one or
both hands in the air.

♪ Tips for teaching the sign for WHERE

○ Play a game with your child: Ask him "WHERE is your TOY (page 126), your SHOE (page 138), our KITTY (page 51)?" You can also play the game with body parts: "Where is your head, your foot, your TUMMY (page 155)?"

○ Ask your child to HELP (page 90) you put away things at the end of the day: "WHERE does our favorite BOOK (page 38) go? WHERE does your teddy BEAR (page 32) go?" Show him how to help you put away the groceries, clean clothes, or unbreakable dishes and utensils from the dishwasher.

○ Talk about where baby animals eat and sleep: BIRDS (page 36) sleep in a TREE (page 154), BABIES (page 27) sleep in cribs (BED, page 34), MOMMY (page 104) and DADDY (page 61) sleep in a BIG (page 164) BED, our KITTY sleeps in a CHAIR (page 54).

♪ Song to sing and sign WHERE

9. White Sheep and Black Sheep (page 212)

SIGN OF SUCCESS

"We used the WHERE sign in the context of 'WHERE is it?' Instead of using the sign of shaking the finger we use a 'natural' gesture. When we want to find something such as shoes, books, or toys, we lift our shoulders, extend our hands palms up with a small movement of the hands moving away from each other, and ask 'Where is it?' as if looking for something. My son sometimes makes this into a game by asking 'Where is it?' of something that he has moved or hidden."

—Carol W.

WINDOW

see Bedtime Bonus Signs (page 170)

YOGURT

see Mealtime Bonus Signs (page 164)

YOU'RE WELCOME

see Mealtime Bonus Signs (page 164)

YUCKY

see BAD (page 28)

YUMMY

see GOOD (page 86)

MEALTIME BONUS SIGNS

Here are a few more signs to use during your child's snack time and mealtime routines.

AGAIN
("Try AGAIN to get the food in your spoon.")

With *one cupped hand* slightly below the other *closed hand* (palm up), move the *cupped hand* up and over the *closed hand* so that fingertips land on palm of *closed hand*.

ALL-GONE

Place side of *open hand* on the flat palm of the other hand. Pull *open hand* to *closed fist* as you pull it away from body.

BAGEL

Tap fingertips of cupped hands together to make a circular shape.

BEANS

Pinch thumb and pointer finger and touch the tip of other extended pointer finger as if snapping off the tip of the bean.

BIB

Tap *gathered fingertips* of one hand to lips. Then outline shape of bib on chest with both pointer fingers, starting at center and moving in upward motion.

BIG

Open hands move away from each other to show a large size.

BOWL

Place *cupped hands* together and then move them apart and upward to outline shape of bowl.

CAKE

Touch fingers of open *cupped hand* to palm of other hand. Lift up *cupped hand* as if cake is rising. (Note: This is the same sign as MUFFIN [page 109]. Sign MUFFIN and say "cake.")

CHOKE

Grasp neck with *cupped hand* with concerned facial expression.

COLD

Shake *closed fists* at shoulders as if shivering from the cold.

COOK

Place back of *closed hand* on upward palm of other hand and then flip closed hand over so that palms are touching.

COOKIE

Place fingertips of *cupped hand* on upward palm of other hand. Twist back and forth as if cutting cookie dough.

CUP

Place little-finger side of *cupped hand* on upward palm of other hand.

DIP

Pinched thumb and pointer finger move down and up as if dipping french fry in ketchup.

DIRTY

Place top of *open hand* under chin and then wiggle fingers.

DON'T-LIKE

Pinch thumb and middle finger in front of chest and pull hand away from body. Then twist wrist and open fingers as if discarding the disliked item.

FAVORITE

Touch middle finger to one side of chin.

FORK

Tap fingertips of *two open fingers* on palm of other hand, twist wrist, and tap again.

FULL

Move *closed hand* up body from stomach to chest as if showing how full you are.

HOT

Place *open hand cupped* in front of mouth. Then rotate hand away from mouth quickly as if food is too hot to eat.

ICE CREAM

Move *closed fist* in front of mouth as if licking an ice cream cone two times.

JUICE

Use extended little finger to draw a *J* at corner of mouth.

LIKE

Pinch thumb and middle finger in front of chest as you pull hand away from body.

LITTLE

Bring palms of *closed hands* close together to indicate a small size.

MINE

Tap *open hand* on chest to indicate possession.

NAPKIN

Use *closed hand* to wipe mouth as you would with napkin.

PIE

Move little-finger side of *closed hand* on palm of other hand to show cutting motion for slicing each side of piece of pie.

PLATE

With *cupped hands* in front of body and palms facing each other, extend and touch tips of middle fingers. Then rock wrists back until thumbs touch to outline shape of plate.

POUR

Move *closed fist* as if holding the handle of a pitcher and pouring the contents into the other *cupped hand*.

PUDDING

See SPOON (page 168)

PUMPKIN

Flick middle finger on back of other *closed hand* as if tapping a pumpkin.

RESTAURANT

Wrap middle finger around pointer finger and move down chin at both sides of mouth.

SANDWICH

Place both *cupped hands* in front of mouth as if holding a sandwich.

SMELL

Brush fingertips of
closed hand over tip of
nose several times.

SPAGHETTI

Extended little fingers of
closed fists draw circle
around each other and
then pull apart.

SPOON

Two closed fingers scoop across
other *cupped hand* (palm up) and up
to mouth two times as if scooping
from bowl. (Note: This is also the
sign for PUDDING and YOGURT.)

STIR

Move *closed fist* in
circular motion as if
stirring with a spoon.

STRAW

Pinch together thumb and pointer
finger of both *open hands*. In front of
chest move one hand upward from
the other to outline length of straw.

SWEET

Fingertips of *closed hand*
brush chin as if wiping
away a sweet treat.

TABLE

Tap *closed hand* on
forearm of other hand.

TASTE

Touch middle finger to
tongue as if tasting food.

THANK YOU

Place fingertips of *closed hand* in
front of lips. Then pull hand down
and away toward the person to
whom you are expressing gratitude.

THIRSTY

Pull pointer finger
down neck.

TOAST

Tap *two open fingers* of
one hand to both sides of
other *open hand*.

TURKEY

Place top of *closed fist* with thumb
and pointer finger extended under
chin and shake hand back and forth
to show turkey's wattle.

VEGETABLE

Place pointer finger of *two
open fingers* on cheek and
twist forward two times.

WAFFLE

Open hands palm down
with thumbs tucked under
overlap at fingers.

YOGURT

See SPOON (page 168)

YOU'RE WELCOME

Place fingertips of *closed hand* in front of lips.
Then, pull hand down and curve into your chest.
(Note: it is perfectly acceptable for babies and toddlers to respond to someone signing
THANK YOU to them by signing THANK YOU in return and eventually saying: "You're welcome!")

BEDTIME BONUS SIGNS

Here are additional signs to incorporate in your daily life as your child transitions from playtime and mealtime to his "night-night" routine. Several signs given here will also be helpful as you begin toilet teaching. Talking about when your child's DIAPER is DRY or DIRTY will help him develop an awareness of how his body works and lead to eventual success. If your child understands words involved in toileting and can follow simple instructions, he may be ready to start toilet teaching in earnest.

BATHROOM

Tuck thumb between pointer and middle fingers and shake hand back and forth.

BEAUTIFUL

Open hand moves in counterclockwise circle in front of face. Draw fingertips together during motion, and stop near chin.

BOAT

Cup two *closed hands* together and move them forward as if floating in the water.

CHANGE

Extend curved pointer fingers from *closed fists* that are touching at fingers. Rotate both hands clockwise as if hands are changing position with each other.

CURTAIN

Move both *open hands* with thumbs touching palms straight down in front of body to "draw" curtains in the air.

DIAPER

Pinch thumb and pointer finger several times at hips to show location of where you pin or tape diaper.

DIRTY

Place top of *open hand* under chin and wiggle fingers.

DOLL

Tap side of bent pointer finger downward on top of nose.

LOTION

Imitate rubbing lotion on hands and arms.

MASSAGE

Squeeze *cupped hands* open and shut as if massaging someone's shoulders.

PACIFIER

Extend and curve pointer finger and thumb. Place side of pointer finger on lips.

ROCK
(in a rocking chair)

With bent pointer and middle fingers and extended thumbs, move arms in "rocking" motion.

ROOM

Hold *closed hands* with thumbs extended and palms facing inward shoulder-width apart to indicate two opposite walls of room. Next, move hands to mark the other two walls of the room with palms facing body.

SCARED

Open hands with palms facing body move toward and away from each other with "scared" facial expression.

SHAMPOO or WASH-HAIR

Move *open cupped hands*
move them back and
forth at sides of head
as if washing hair.

TIME (for bed)

Tap bent pointer finger
on top of wrist as
if touching wristwatch.

TOWEL

Move *closed fists*
near shoulders as if drying
your back with towel.

WAKE

Flick open thumbs
and pointer fingers placed
at the corner of each eye
as if eyes are opening.

WET

Touch side of mouth
with middle fingers of both
open hands, then gently
open and close gathered
fingertips twice.

WINDOW

With palms facing body,
put the little finger of one
closed hand on top of the
pointer finger of other *closed
hand*. Move top hand up
and down as if window is
opening and closing.

LULLABY BONUS SIGNS

Here are a few rare and appealing signed words your child will love because they occur in the lyrics of the bonus lullabies. I have also added other vocabulary words contained in our bonus lullaby lyrics that may be of interest to your family, such as sister, brother, grandmother, and grandfather.

BARNYARD/FARM

Place thumb of *open hand* on one side of chin and then drag it under to other side.

BASEBALL

Both hands hold imaginary bat and swing it back and forth over shoulder.

BROTHER

PLUS

Gather fingertips of one hand at forehead as if holding baseball cap bill. Then bring pointer fingers of both hands together side by side.

CLIMB

Move hands as if climbing a ladder.

DREAM

Pointer finger bends and straightens as it moves up and away from temple.

GRANDMA

With thumb of *open hand* on chin, move hand up and away from chin in two circular motions.

GRANDPA

With thumb of *open hand* on forehead, move hand up and away from forehead in two circular motions.

PARK

PLUS

Extend thumb and little finger of both closed fists and twist both at wrist. Then place thumb between *two open fingers* on both hands. Touch tips of middle fingers together, curve apart, and curve back together, making a circle with the movement.

PIRATE

Place four *closed fingers* over eye with fingertips toward nose.

PLANE

"Fly" *open hand* with ring and middle fingers folded down in upward direction.

RAINBOW

Open hand with thumb on inward-facing palm draws rainbow over head.

READ

Tips of *two open fingers* swing back and forth near sideways-turned palm of other hand as if eyes scanning a page.

ROLLER COASTER

Curve *closed hand* up and down in front of body as if moving along track.

SEA

Open hands with palms down move up and down away from the body to illustrate waves in the sea.

SISTER

PLUS

Drag thumb down jaw. Then bring pointer fingers of both hands together side by side.

SPIDER

Cupped open hands cross at wrists. Wiggle fingers and move hands forward as if spider is walking.

SWIM

Arms with *cupped closed hands* move as if swimming breaststroke.

TRACTOR

Hands grasp large steering wheel and pretend to drive.

TRAIN/RAILROAD

Form two *closed fingers* palms down with both hands. Place one on top of other and slide fingers on top back and forth.

MEALTIME AND BEDTIME SONGBOOK

SONGS TO SING AND SIGN

MEALTIME SONGS

1. **My Kitchen Door (Music and lyrics by Anne Meeker Miller)**
   APPLE, BIRD, BREAD, CAT, CEREAL, CHEESE, DANCE, DOG, DUCK, EAT/FOOD, FRUIT, GIRL, GIVE, HUNGRY, MEAT, MILK, MORE, MOUSE, PIG, PLEASE

2. **Crawly, Creepy Little Mousie (Collected by Pete Seeger/Additional verses by Anne Meeker Miller)**
   BOY, BUG, CHEESE, CRACKER, EAT/NIBBLE, FRUIT, HELP, MOUSE, PLAY/TOY

3. **The Muffin Man (Traditional/Arranged by Anne Meeker Miller)**
   BREAD, CHEESE, CRACKER, DADDY, DRINK, EAT, FINE, FRUIT, GOOD/YUMMY, HUNGRY, LOVE, MILK, MUFFIN, PEACH, PEAR, STORE, TUMMY, UP

4. **Fill the Basket (Music and lyrics by Anne Meeker Miller)**
ALL-DONE, APPLE, BANANA, CARROT, EAT, FILL, FRIEND, GRAPES, MORE, MUSIC, ORANGE, PEACH, PEAR, PEAS, PLAY, PLEASE, STOP, TOMATO, WANT

5. **John the Rabbit (Traditional/Arranged by Anne Meeker Miller)**
BAD, BANANA, CARROT, CORN, DIG, EAT/FOOD, FRUIT, HIDE, MORE, MUSIC, PLAY, POTATO, RABBIT, STORE, TOMATO, TREE

BEDTIME SONGS

6. **What Did You Have for Your Supper? (Traditional/Arranged by Anne Meeker Miller)**
BABY, BED/SLEEP, CARROT, CHAIR, DRINK, EAT/SUPPER, LOVE, MEAT, MOMMY, MUSIC/SONG, NOODLES, PEACH, PRAYER, TIRED, WANT, WATER

7. **Mister Moon (Traditional/Arranged by Rob Mathieu and Anne Meeker Miller)**
ALL-DONE, DOWN, HAPPY, HIDE, LIGHT-OFF, LOVE, MOON, NIGHT-NIGHT, PLAY, PLEASE, SUN, TREE, UP

8. **We're Having a Bath (Music and lyrics by Zoe Miller, Rick Burch, and Anne Meeker Miller)**
BATH/WASH, BEAR, BED, BRUSH-TEETH, BUBBLE, COMB-HAIR, DADDY, DANCE, DRY, FINE/ALRIGHT, HAPPY, NIGHT-NIGHT, PANTS, SHIRT, SHOES, SOAP, SOCKS

9. **White Sheep and Black Sheep (Based on the poem "Clouds" by Christina Rosetti/Music and lyrics by Anne Meeker Miller)**
BABY, BED/SLEEP, BIRD, BUTTERFLY, FLOWER, GO, HOME, LIGHT-OFF, LOVE/HOLD/SNUGGLE, NIGHT-NIGHT, SHEEP, SMILE, STOP, TREE, UP, WALK, WHERE?

10. What'll We Do with the Baby? (Traditional/Arranged by Anne Meeker Miller)
BABY, BATH/WASH, BED, BLANKET, DADDY, DRINK, EAT/FEED, GIVE, KISS, LOVE, MEAT, MUSIC/SING, PAJAMAS, PLAY, POTATO, ROOSTER, SOAP, SPLASH

LULLABIES TO SING AND SHARE WITH YOUR CHILD

11. Rainbows, Railroads, and Rhymes (Music and lyrics by Rick Burch)
ALL-DONE, BED, BLANKET, CHAIR, DANCE, FLOWER, KISS, LIGHT-OFF, LOVE/HOLD/HUG, MOMMY, MUSIC/SING, NIGHT-NIGHT, PLAY
Lullaby Bonus Words: *barnyard, baseball, pirate, plane, rainbow, read, rock (in rocking chair), spider, tractor, train/railroad*

12. Now I Lay Me Down to Sleep (Music by Jennifer Maddox and Anne Meeker Miller/Lyrics by Anne Meeker Miller) 🌙
APPLE, BED/SLEEP, DADDY, DARK, FINE/ALRIGHT, LOVE, MOMMY, PLAY, PRAY, STAR, TREE
Lullaby Bonus Words: *brother, climb, dream, grandma, park, pie, sea, sister, swim, roller coaster*

MEALTIME SONGS

MY KITCHEN DOOR

(Music and lyrics by Anne Meeker Miller)

Words to sing and sign:
**APPLE, BIRD, BREAD, CAT, CEREAL, CHEESE, DANCE,
DOG, DUCK, EAT/FOOD, FRUIT, GIRL, GIVE, HUNGRY,
MEAT, MILK, MORE, MOUSE, PIG, PLEASE**

Babies and toddlers love animals and the sounds they make. I invited all kinds of critters into this musical "kitchen" so that your child could watch them eat while he sat in his high chair and enjoyed his own snack. Singing this story is a lot less messy than actually feeding a menagerie in your kitchen. And the built-in repetition provides great practice of mealtime vocabulary.

Sign suggestions to accompany the song

Verse 1.

Oh a **mouse** snuck in my kitchen door,	Sign MOUSE
He **ate** some **food (eat)** and asked for **more**,	Sign EAT or MORE
The **mouse** was very **hungry**,	Sign MOUSE or HUNGRY
So I **gave** him some **cheese**.	Sign GIVE or CHEESE

Verse 2.

Oh, a **bird** flew in my kitchen door,	Sign BIRD
He **ate** some **food (eat)** and asked for **more**,	Sign EAT or MORE
The **bird** was very **hungry**,	Sign BIRD or HUNGRY
So I **gave** him some **fruit**.	Sign GIVE or FRUIT

Verse 3.

Oh, a **duck** waddled in my kitchen door,	Sign DUCK
He **ate** some **food (eat)** and asked for **more**,	Sign EAT or MORE
The **duck** was very, very **hungry**	Sign DUCK or HUNGRY
So I **gave** him some **bread**.	Sign GIVE or BREAD

Verse 4.

Oh, a **cat** strolled in my kitchen door,   Sign CAT

He **ate** some **food (eat)** and asked for **more**,   Sign EAT or MORE

The **cat** was very **hungry**,   Sign CAT or HUNGRY

So I **gave** him some **milk**.   Sign GIVE or MILK

Verse 5.

Oh, a **dog** ran in my kitchen door,   Sign DOG

He ate some **food (eat)** and asked for **more**,   Sign EAT or MORE

The **dog** was very **hungry**,   Sign DOG or HUNGRY

So I **gave** him some **meat**.   Sign GIVE or MEAT

Verse 6.

Oh, a **pig** marched in my kitchen door,   Sign PIG

He ate some **food (eat)** and asked for **more**,   Sign EAT or MORE

The **pig** was very, very,   Sign PIG

very, very **hungry**,   Sign HUNGRY

So I **gave** him some **cereal**.   Sign GIVE or CEREAL

Verse 7.

Oh, a **girl danced** in my kitchen door,   Sign GIRL or DANCE

She ate some **food (eat)** and asked for **more**,   Sign EAT or MORE

The **girl** was very, very **hungry**,   Sign GIRL or HUNGRY

So I'll **give** her an **apple** and **cheese**   Sign GIVE or APPLE or CHEESE

If she'll just say "**Please!**"   Sign PLEASE

MY KITCHEN DOOR

CRAWLY, CREEPY LITTLE MOUSIE

(Collected by Pete Seeger/Additional verses by Anne Meeker Miller)

Words to sing and sign:
BOY, BUG, CHEESE, CRACKER, EAT/NIBBLE, FRUIT, HELP, MOUSE, PLAY/TOY

I enjoyed several wonderful phone conversations with the "Father of Folk Music," Mr. Pete Seeger. He and I talked about my work combining music and sign language for young children. "Old Pete" sang me a children's rhyme set to a march from the American Revolutionary War. The rhyme in many variations may be familiar as a game passed down through generations of families. When used as a "tickle," parents or grandparents gently brushed baby's hand with their fingertips and moved their tickle up the child's arm to under his chin. The directions for our "tickle" song as well as sign language are given here. I am joined by Konza Swamp, one of the premiere bluegrass bands in the Midwest.

Sign and play suggestions to accompany the song

Verse 1.
Crawly, creepy little **mousie**,
From the barney to the housie,
In the pantry under the shelf,
He found some **cheese**,
And **helped** himself.
Nibble, nibble, nibble, nibble.
Nibble, nibble, nibble, nibble,
Nibble, nibble, nibble, nibble.
Nibble (eat)!

Sign MOUSE
Walk fingers up child's arm or tummy
Tickle child under the chin
Sign CHEESE
Sign HELP
Sign EAT on self or child

Verse 2.
Black and shiny little **buggie**,   Sign BUG
From the garden under the ruggie,   Walk fingers up child's arm or tummy
In the pantry under the shelf,   Tickle child under the chin
He found some **crackers**,   Sign CRACKER
And **helped** himself,   Sign HELP
Nibble, nibble, nibble, nibble . . .   Sign EAT on self or child
Nibble (eat)!

Verse 3.
Curly-headed little **boy**,   Sign BOY
He crawled to find   Walk fingers up child's arm or tummy
His favorite **toy**,   Continue walking fingers or sign
          PLAY/TOY
He looked in the pantry under the shelf,   Tickle child under the chin
He found some **fruit**,   Sign FRUIT
And **helped** himself,   Sign HELP
Nibble, nibble, nibble, nibble . . .   Sign EAT on self or child
Nibble (eat)!

CRAWLY, CREEPY LITTLE MOUSIE

Traditional / Additional verses by Anne Meeker Miller

THE MUFFIN MAN

(Traditional/Arranged by Anne Meeker Miller)

Words to sing and sign:
**BREAD, CHEESE, CRACKER, DADDY, DRINK, EAT,
FINE, FRUIT, GOOD/YUMMY, HUNGRY, LOVE, MILK,
MUFFIN, PEACH, PEAR, STORE, TUMMY, UP**

I love this old children's song but have always wanted to know more about the mysterious Man of Muffins: Did he have a Muffin Wife and Muffin Babies? And did he sell anything else besides muffins? I incorporated jazz elements in this song, as well as a surprise ending!

	Sign suggestions to accompany the song
Hey there, boys, it's time to **eat**	Sign EAT
Let's visit the man with the **yummy (good)** treats.	Sign YUMMY
Do you know the **Muffin** Man, the **Muffin** Man, the **Muffin** Man?	Sign MUFFIN
Do you know the **Muffin** Man who lives on Drury Lane?	Sign MUFFIN
Yes, I know the **Muffin** Man, the **Muffin** Man, the **Muffin** Man,	Sign MUFFIN
Oh yes, I know the **Muffin** Man who lives on Drury Lane.	Sign MUFFIN
Verse 1.	
He makes his **muffins** fresh each day,	Sign MUFFIN
And then he stacks them **up.**	Sign UP
I love that fellow's ice cold **milk**.	Sign MILK

I **drink** it from a cup!	Sign DRINK
You should know the **Muffin** Man, the	Sign MUFFIN
Muffin Man, the **Muffin** Man . . .	
Oh yes, we know the **Muffin** Man, the **Muffin**	Sign MUFFIN
Man, the **Muffin** Man . . .	

Verse 2.

He sells his **crackers** by the bag.	Sign CRACKERS
His **cheese** is really **yummy**.	Sign CHEESE or YUMMY
I like to **eat** his fresh baked **bread**.	Sign EAT or BREAD
It warms my little **tummy**!	Sign TUMMY
You should know the **Muffin** Man, the	Sign MUFFIN
Muffin Man, that **Muffin** Man . . .	
Yes, we know the **Muffin** Man, the **Muffin** Man,	Sign MUFFIN
the **Muffin** Man . . .	

Verse 3.

His **store** is always full of folks	Sign STORE
Who're **hungry** as can be!	Sign HUNGRY
They choose some **pears** and **peaches**, too.	Sign PEAR or PEACH or FRUIT
Please save some **fruit** for me!	Sign FRUIT
You should know the **Muffin** man, the **Muffin**	Sign MUFFIN
man, the **Muffin** man . . .	

Verse 4.

How I **love** that man.	Sign LOVE
I **love** him like a little child can.	Sign LOVE
He's my **daddy** and he's so **fine**.	Sign DADDY or FINE
The **muffin** and the man are mine, all mine!	Sign MUFFIN
Oh, we live, live, live, live,	
Yes, we live on a lane called Drury Lane.	

THE MUFFIN MAN

FILL THE BASKET

(Music and lyrics by Anne Meeker Miller)

Words to sing and sign:
ALL-DONE, APPLE, BANANA, CARROT, EAT, FILL, FRIEND, GRAPES, MORE, MUSIC, ORANGE, PEACH, PEAR, PEAS, PLAY, PLEASE, STOP, TOMATO, WANT

It is curious when people praise your child for being a good eater, but that was the compliment I received often on behalf of my son Kevin and his great enthusiasm for fruits and vegetables. I created this little ditty to give my students—and my own children—the opportunity to choose the fresh produce they would like to eat. It also helps practice "Yes, PLEASE" and "ALL-DONE," two valuable mealtime messages.

Sign suggestions to accompany the song

Fill the basket to the top.	Sign FILL
Fill the basket to the top.	Sign FILL
Time to **eat**	Sign EAT
So please don't **stop**!	Sign STOP
Fill the basket to the top.	Sign FILL
Verse 1.	
Do you **want banana**?	Sign WANT or BANANA
Yes, **please**! Yes, **please**!	Sign PLEASE
Do you **want** an **orange**?	Sign WANT or ORANGE
Yes, **please**! Yes, **please**!	Sign PLEASE
Do you **want** an **apple**?	Sign WANT or APPLE
Yes, **please**! Yes, **please**!	Sign PLEASE
All done! All done!	Sign ALL-DONE
Time to **play**! Time to **play**!	Sign PLAY
Then it's time to fill the basket to the . . .	Sign FILL

Verse 2.

Do you **want** a **peach**?	Sign WANT or PEACH
Yes, **please**! Yes, **please**!	Sign PLEASE
Do you **want** some **grapes**?	Sign WANT or GRAPES
Yes, **please**! Yes, **please**!	Sign PLEASE
Do you **want** a **pear**?	Sign WANT or PEAR
Yes, **please**! Yes, **please**!	Sign PLEASE
All done! All done!	Sign ALL-DONE
Time to **play**! Time to **play**!	Sign PLAY
Then it's time to . . .	

Verse 3.

Do you **want tomatoes**?	Sign WANT or TOMATO
Yes, **please**! Yes, **please**!	Sign PLEASE
Do you **want** some **carrots**?	Sign WANT or CARROT
Yes, **please**! Yes, **please**!	Sign PLEASE
Do you **want** some **peas**?	Sign WANT or PEAS
Yes, **please**! Yes, **please**!	Sign PLEASE
All done! All done!	Sign ALL-DONE
Time to **play**! Time to **play**!	Sign PLAY
Then it's time to . . .	

Verse 4.

Fill the basket one **more** time.	Sign FILL or MORE
I will share with these **friends** of mine.	Sign FRIEND
How we love *Baby Sing and Sign!* (**music**)!	Sign MUSIC
Fill the basket to the . . .	Sign FILL
To the top!	Sign FILL

JOHN THE RABBIT

(Traditional/Arranged by Anne Meeker Miller)

Words to sing and sign:
**BAD, BANANA, CARROT, CORN, DIG, EAT/FOOD, FRUIT, HIDE,
MORE, MUSIC, PLAY, POTATO, RABBIT, STORE, TOMATO, TREE**

"John the Rabbit" is a wonderful old call-and-response song about a naughty rabbit that gobbles out of the garden. The narrator sings the story, and the chorus responds with an enthusiastic "Oh, yes!" My students absolutely love this song; I give them each a turn creating their own verse by suggesting a food that John might have eaten from their garden. One little boy could never seem to retain information he learned in preschool and apply it to new situations. I taught his class this song shortly before they were to visit the pumpkin patch. The owner of the pumpkin farm told the children a story about how he would have had a much larger crop if the rabbits and other animals had left his plants alone. Jake exclaimed: "Oh no, it was John the Rabbit." This is one of a hundred stories I could share where I was reminded that music profoundly affects a child's ability to learn and grow.

Sign suggestions to accompany the song

Verse 1.
Oh, John the **Rabbit** (Oh, yes!)	Sign RABBIT
Oh, John the **Rabbit** (Oh, yes!)	Sign RABBIT
Had a mighty **bad** habit (Oh, yes!)	Sign BAD
Of **digging** in my garden. (Oh, yes!)	Sign DIG
He ate **tomatoes** (Oh, yes!)	Sign TOMATO
And sweet, sweet **potatoes.** (Oh, yes!)	Sign POTATO
And if he **hides** (Oh, yes!)	Sign HIDE
Out under my **tree**, (Oh, yes!)	Sign TREE

There'll be no **food (eat)** (Oh, yes!)	Sign EAT
For you and for me! (Oh, yes!)	Point to other and then to self
Verse 2.	
Oh, John the **Rabbit** (Oh, yes!)	Sign RABBIT
Oh, John, John the **Rabbit** (Oh, yes!)	Sign RABBIT
Had a mighty **bad** habit (Oh, yes!)	Sign BAD
Of **playing** in my pantry. (Oh, yes!)	Sign PLAY
He ate **bananas** (Oh, yes!)	Sign BANANA
I bought at the **store**. (Oh, yes!)	Sign STORE
He ate two **carrots**, (Oh, yes!)	Sign CARROT
And then he ate lots **more**. (Oh, yes!)	Sign MORE
And if he **hides** (Oh, yes!)	Sign HIDE
Outside my door, (Oh, yes!)	
I won't **dig** (Oh, yes!)	Sign DIG
A garden no **more.** (Oh, yes!)	Sign MORE
He ate some **fruit**,	Sign FRUIT
And then he **played** the flute (**music**).	Sign PLAY or MUSIC
He ate some **corn**,	Sign CORN
And then he **played** the horn (**music**).	Sign PLAY or MUSIC
Oh, John the **Rabbit** . . . there'll be no food	Sign RABBIT
For you and for me (for you and for me),	Point to other and then to self
For you and for me (for you and for me),	Point to other and then to self
For you and for me (for you and for me),	Point to other and then to self
For you and for me.	Point to other and then to self
(**Potatoes, tomatoes,**	Sign POTATO or TOMATO
Carrots and **more,**	Sign CARROT or MORE
Bananas and **fruit**	Sign BANANA or FRUIT
I bought at the **store**)	Sign STORE
Oh, John the **Rabbit**.	Sign RABBIT
(Oh, yeah!)	

JOHN THE RABBIT

Traditional/Arranged by Anne Meeker Miller

BEDTIME SONGS

WHAT DID YOU HAVE FOR YOUR SUPPER?

(Traditional/Arranged by Anne Meeker Miller)

Words to sing and sign:
BABY, BED/SLEEP, CARROT, CHAIR, DRINK, EAT/SUPPER, LOVE, MEAT, MOMMY, MUSIC/SONG, NOODLES, PEACH, PRAYER, TIRED, WANT, WATER

(Note: place fingertips of cupped hands on chest, then roll hands forward and slump shoulders as if fatigued for the TIRED sign; you may also choose to use BED instead of TIRED with your child)

This old ballad is also known as "Lord Randall," "Jimmy Randal," and "The Croodlin Doo," to name a few alternate versions. It may have originated as an Italian ballad in the 1600s. It is a familiar ditty throughout the British Isles as well as North America. The original lyrics tell the story of a fellow who was poisoned when he ate eel soup for supper! We offer some tastier—and less hazardous—fair. The strong meter and harmonies of this tune make it a perfect dance for you and your baby. Take her for a spin around your living room after supper.

Sign suggestions to accompany the song

Verse 1.
It's what did you have
for your **supper (eat)**,   Sign EAT
Little **baby**, my **love**?   Sign BABY or LOVE
Oh, what did you have for your **supper (eat)**,   Sign EAT
my own little one (**love**)?   Sign LOVE
Some *meat* and ripe **peaches**,   Sign MEAT or PEACH
Mama, make my **bed** soon,   Sign MOMMY or BED

For I'm **tired** from my day,	Sign TIRED or BED
And I **want** to lie down (**bed**).	Sign WANT or BED
Verse 2.	
. . . . *Noodles* and *carrots* . . .	Sign NOODLES or CARROT
Verse 3.	
. . . . A cool *drink* of *water* . . .	Sign DRINK or WATER
Verse 4.	
It's what did you have after **supper** (**eat**)	Sign EAT
my **baby**, my **love**?	Sign BABY or LOVE
Oh, what did you have after **supper** (**eat**),	Sign EAT
my own little one (**love**)?	Sign LOVE
A **song** (**music**) and a **prayer**	Sign MUSIC or PRAYER
In your favorite **chair**.	Sign CHAIR
You are **tired** from your day,	Sign TIRED or BED
And you **want** to lie down (**bed**).	Sign WANT or BED
I am **tired** from my day,	Sign TIRED or BED
And I **want** to lie down (**bed**).	Sign WANT or BED

WHAT DID YOU HAVE FOR YOUR SUPPER?

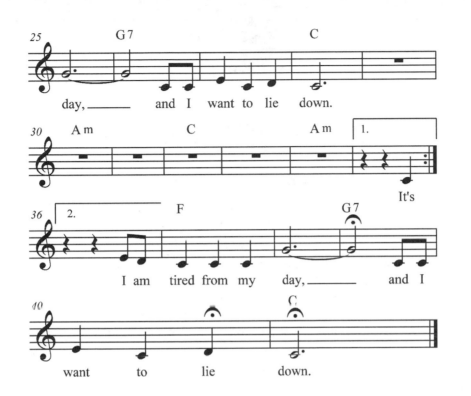

25   **G 7**   **C**

day, _____ and I want to lie down.

30   **A m**   **C**   **A m**   **1.**

It's

36   **2.**   **F**   **G 7**

I am tired from my day, _____ and I

40   **C**

want to lie down.

Traditional / Additional verses by Anne Meeker Miller

MISTER MOON

(Traditional/Arranged by Rob Mathieu and Anne Meeker Miller)

Words to sing and sign:

**ALL-DONE, DOWN, HAPPY, HIDE, LIGHT-OFF, LOVE, MOON,
NIGHT-NIGHT, PLAY, PLEASE, SUN, TREE, UP**

My son, Andy, had a fascination with the moon from the get-go. "Moon" was one of his first spoken words. My mother sang "Mister Moon" to me as a child. I have added equal time for "Lady Sun" in my arrangement. I am joined on the music CD by the award-winning barber-shop quartet, Quadio.

	Sign suggestions to accompany the song
Sun and **moon** are always around.	Sign SUN or MOON
How I **love** their shining.	Sign LOVE
When one's **up**	Sign UP
The other is **down**.	Sign DOWN
Which one will it be?	Sign UP and DOWN at the same time!
Verse 1.	
Oh, Mister **Moon, moon**,	Sign MOON
Bright 'n' silv'ry **moon**,	Sign MOON
Won't you **please** shine down on me?	Sign PLEASE
Oh, Mister **Moon, moon**,	Sign MOON
Bright 'n' silv'ry **moon**,	Sign MOON
Hiding behind that **tree**.	Sign HIDE or TREE
When **sun** is shining,	Sign SUN
It's time for **play**,	Sign PLAY
But when the **moon** shines,	Sign MOON

We're done (**all-done**) with day.	Sign ALL-DONE
Oh, Mister **Moon, moon,**	Sign MOON
Bright 'n' silv'ry **moon,**	Sign MOON
Won't you **please** shine down on me?	Sign PLEASE
Verse 2.	
Oh, Lady **Sun, sun,**	Sign SUN
Warm and yellow **sun,**	Sign SUN
Won't you **please** shine down on me?	Sign PLEASE
Oh, Lady **Sun, sun,**	Sign SUN
Warm and yellow **sun,**	Sign SUN
Happy as you can be,	Sign HAPPY
When **moon** is rising,	Sign MOON
Sun says, "**Good-night!**"	Sign SUN or NIGHT-NIGHT
Closes her eyes,	Close your eyes or touch them!
And **turns off her light.**	Sign LIGHT-OFF
Oh, Lady **Sun, sun,**	Sign SUN
Warm and yellow **sun,**	Sign SUN
Won't you **please** shine down on me?	Sign PLEASE
Oh, Mister Moon . . .	
. . . Won't you **please** shine down on?	Sign PLEASE
Talk about your shine on (**moon**),	Sign MOON
Please shine down on me?	Sign PLEASE

MISTER MOON

Traditional/Arranged by Rob Mathieu and Anne Meeker Miller

WE'RE HAVING A BATH

(Music and lyrics by Zoe Miller, Rick Burch, and Anne Meeker Miller)

Words to sing and sign:
**BATH/WASH, BEAR, BED, BRUSH-TEETH, BUBBLE, COMB-HAIR,
DADDY, DANCE, DRY, FINE/ALRIGHT, HAPPY, NIGHT-NIGHT,
PANTS, SHIRT, SHOES, SOAP, SOCKS**

My friend Zoe Miller embraced motherhood with gusto, so it didn't surprise me in the slightest when she called to share the bathtub song she created for her baby daughter, Augusta Anne. I will never erase her premiere performance of "We're Having a Bath" from my cell phone voicemail box. With her blessing, fellow songwriter Rick Burch and I have re-arranged and embellished her authentic bathtub theme. We welcome any new verses or variations you would like to add. You will have plenty of musical inspiration while sponging your little sweetie in the tub.

Sign suggestions to accompany the song

We're having a **bath**.	Sign BATH
Yeah, we're having a **bath**.	Sign BATH
We're having a sudsy, **bubbly bath**.	Sign BUBBLE or BATH
We're having a **bath**, yeah, we're having a **bath**.	Sign BATH
We're having a sudsy, **bubbly bath**.	Sign BUBBLE or BATH
Verse 1.	
We take off our **shirts** now.	Sign SHIRT
We take off our **pants**.	Sign PANTS
We're doing our **happy**	Sign HAPPY
Bubbly dance!	Sign BUBBLE or DANCE
We're grabbing the **soap** now.	Sign SOAP

We're ready to rock (**dance**).	Sign DANCE
We take off our **shoes** and	Sign SHOES
We take off our **socks**!	Sign SOCKS
Verse 2.	
We're **washing (bath)** our fingers.	Sign BATH or wiggle fingers
We're **washing (bath)** our toes.	Sign BATH or touch toes
We're **washing (bath)** our legs now.	Sign BATH or touch legs
We're **washing (bath)** our nose.	Sign BATH or touch nose
We're **washing (bath)** our bottoms.	Sign BATH or touch bottom
We're **washing (bath)** our tops.	Sign BATH or touch tummy
We're **washing (bath)** our arms now,	Sign BATH or touch arms
And we're **washing (bath)** our "mops" (hair)!	Sign BATH or touch hair
We're out of the **bath**.	Sign BATH
Yeah, we're out of the **bath**.	Sign BATH
We're out of the sudsy, **bubbly bath**.	Sign BUBBLE or BATH
We're **drying** our fingers.	Sign DRY or wiggle fingers
We're **drying** our toes.	Sign DRY or touch toes
We're **drying** our legs,	Sign DRY or touch legs
And we're **drying** our nose.	Sign DRY or touch nose
We're **brushing our teeth** now.	Sign BRUSH-TEETH
We're **combing our hair**.	Sign COMB-HAIR
We're grabbing our **daddy**.	Sign DADDY
We're grabbing our **bear**!	Sign BEAR
We're into our **bed** now.	Sign BED
We're feeling **alright (fine)**.	Sign FINE
It's time for us to say:	
"Night-night!"	Sign NIGHT-NIGHT

WE'RE HAVING A BATH

WHITE SHEEP AND BLACK SHEEP

(Based on the poem "Clouds" by Christina Rosetti/Music and lyrics by Anne Meeker Miller)

> "White sheep, white sheep, on a blue hill,
> When the wind stops, you all stand still,
> When the wind blows, you walk away slow,
> White sheep, white sheep, where do you go?
> —"Clouds" by Christina Rosetti (1830–1894)

Words to sing and sign:
**BABY, BED/SLEEP, BIRD, BUTTERFLY, FLOWER, GO, HOME,
LIGHT-OFF, LOVE/HOLD/SNUGGLE, NIGHT-NIGHT, SHEEP,
SMILE, STOP, TREE, UP, WALK, WHERE**

Music is an intriguing combination of sound and silence. The beauty of this tune is in the quiet it contains. I use this song to teach the concept of sound and silence as well as the word STOP. The moment your child hears the word STOP, the music ends for a few seconds. I have varied the length of the silent interludes so that your child won't be able to anticipate their duration right away. Watch his face as you play the song and see if he gives you a curious look when the music disappears and then suddenly resumes. Watch him as he listens intently at the conclusion of the song. Where did those sheep go?

Sign suggestions to accompany the song

Verse 1.
White **sheep** and black **sheep**   Sign SHEEP
Walk on a hill.   Sign WALK

When the wind **stops**, you all stand still.	Sign STOP
When the wind blows, you **walk** away slow.	Sign WALK
White **sheep** and black **sheep**,	Sign SHEEP
Where do you go?	Sign WHERE?
Verse 2.	
Birdie, sweet **birdie**,	Sign BIRD
Snug (love) in his nest.	Sign LOVE
When the wind **stops**,	Sign STOP
It's time to rest **(bed)**.	Sign BED
When the wind blows, you fly **home** to me.	Sign HOME
Birdie, sweet **birdie**,	Sign BIRD
High in the **tree**.	Sign TREE
Verse 3.	
Butterfly, oh **butterfly**,	Sign BUTTERFLY
Up in the sky. **Up** in the sky	Sign UP or lift BUTTERFLY sign
When the wind **stops**, you gently glide.	Sign STOP
When the wind blows **(go)**, a **flower** you see.	Sign GO or FLOWER
Butterfly, oh **butterfly**,	Sign BUTTERFLY
Where can you be?	Sign WHERE?
Verse 4.	
Baby, my **baby**,	Sign BABY
Time for **good-night**.	Sign NIGHT-NIGHT
When the wind **stops**,	Sign STOP
Turn off your light **(light off)**.	Sign LIGHT-OFF
When the wind blows, I'll **hold (love)**	Sign LOVE
you awhile.	
Baby, my **baby**,	Sign BABY
Sheep and **birds** and **butterflies**,	Sign SHEEP or BIRD or BUTTERFLY
And anything to make you **smile**.	Sign SMILE

WHITE SHEEP AND BLACK SHEEP

WHAT'LL WE DO WITH THE BABY?

(Traditional/Arranged by Anne Meeker Miller)

Words to sing and sign:
**BABY, BATH/WASH, BED, BLANKET, DADDY, DRINK, EAT/FEED,
GIVE, KISS, LOVE, MEAT, MUSIC/SING, PAJAMAS, PLAY,
POTATO, ROOSTER, SOAP, SPLASH**

(Note: direct your gathered fingertips away from your body to sign FEED instead of to your lips as you would for the EAT sign)

"What'll We Do with the Baby?" is from the folk music collection of Cecil J. Sharp (1859–1924). Born in London, Sharp devoted most of his career to musical pursuits, collecting English traditional dances and folk music. A teacher and composer, he traveled to the United States in 1916 to collect folk songs from remote regions of the Appalachian Mountains. He researched the transformation of English folk songs he collected in rural England as they were performed by new generations of immigrants here in America.

This song would make a great "bounce" for your toddler. Position your child on your knees and hold his hands as you sing and gently bounce him to the beat. You can also make up your own verses, adding all of your child's favorite activities. Here are some suggestions: "EAT (page 73) a snack of GRAPE-ios (page 88) . . . say 'NIGHT-NIGHT' (page 114) to the BIRD-ios (page 36) . . . HELP (page 90) put away my DIRTY (page 171) clothes." The baby humor and consequent interest in the tune has more to do with the funny "ee-oh" ending you add to his familiar vocabulary words than with the actions themselves. It has the same appeal as the repeating "Ee-I-Ee-I-Oh" stanza in "Old MacDonald's Farm." Make sure you share your silly self with your child as you perform the song with great animation for his amusement!

Verse 1.

What'll we do with the **baby**?	Sign BABY
What'll we do with the **baby**?	Sign BABY
What'll we do with the **baby**?	Sign BABY
Oh, we'll **feed** it	Sign FEED
Meat and **potato**.	Sign MEAT or POTATO
Feed it	Sign FEED
Meat and **potato**.	Sign MEAT or POTATO
And now it's off to **bed** you go!	Sign BED

Verse 2.

What'll we do with the **baby**? . . .	Sign BABY
. . . Oh, we'll give that babe a **bath**-ee-oh . . .	Sign BATH
And **wash** (**bath**) it	Sign BATH
With sweet **soap**-ee-oh.	Sign SOAP or BATH

Verse 3.

What'll we do with the **baby**? . . .	Sign BABY
. . . Oh, we'll let it **play** and **splash**-ee-oh . . .	Sign PLAY or SPLASH
. . . Then dress it in some **jammy-ee-ohs** (**pajamas**).	Sign PAJAMAS

Verse 4.

What'll we do with the **baby**? . . .   Sign BABY

. . . Oh, we'll wrap it up in a **blank-ee-oh**   Sign BLANKET
   (**blanket**).

. . . And send it to its **Daddy**-oh!   Sign DADDY

Verse 5.

What'll we do with the **baby**? . . .   Sign BABY

. . . We'll **give** it a **drink**   Sign GIVE or DRINK

And we'll **kiss** its toes . . .   Sign KISS

And now it's off to **bed** you go!   Sign BED

Verse 6.

What'll we do with the **baby**? . . .   Sign BABY

. . . Oh, we'll **sing** to it   Sign SING

"I **love** you so . . .   Sign LOVE

I'll see you when the **rooster** crows!"   Sign ROOSTER

And that's what we'll do with the **baby**!   Sign BABY

From *Folk Songs of the Southern Appalachians*

Collected by Cecil J. Sharp and Edited by Maud Karpeles

Copyright © 1932 by Oxford University Press

Used by permission. All rights reserved.

Arranged by Anne Meeker Miller

WHAT'LL WE DO WITH THE BABY?

LULLABIES TO SING AND SHARE WITH YOUR CHILD

Lullabies are the ultimate communication experience between you and your child. Parents can express the depth of their love and affection for their child in a way that only music makes possible. As you listen together or as you softly sing to your child, you are creating a bond that will last a lifetime, not unlike the photo albums that you open and share together to reminisce about those first months of your new "friendship" as parent and child. My children and I still sing the lullabies of their babyhood on occasion. These songs will be the same ones my sons will sing to their babies.

You might incorporate these two bonus lullabies as a part of your child's bedtime routine. Perhaps you can place a CD player in her room and play your *Mealtime and Bedtime* music CD after reading books and before you put her into her crib or bed. The last lullaby purposefully includes gentle instrumental music to provide the perfect segue to slumber.

Many of the signs included in the *Mealtime and Bedtime* dictionary are used in the bonus lullabies. Some babies may be distracted from their enjoyment of the songs if you sign along, but your baby may enjoy watching your fingers "sing" the song as she sits in your lap with her back to your chest. She may even place her hands on top of yours to "sing along" with you. You know your child best. However, it is fine to set aside language learning to focus on the bonding benefits of sharing a lullaby and snuggling with your baby in those precious moments before she goes to sleep.

The bonus lullabies contain some unusual words—such as "pirate" and "pie"—that your child may not hear in everyday conversation with you (see Lullaby Signs, pages 173–175). As parents, we frequently communicate using short repetitive phrases with babies to make our point: "All-done with lunch . . . time to play . . . be sweet to Kitty-Cat." However, there are thousands of words not frequently used with babies and toddlers that they need to hear and comprehend before they head for preschool.

The good news is that singing and reading aloud to children achieves this goal. The imagery, stories, and varied vocabulary of music and books immerses the child in a language-rich world. Through music and books, children vicariously experience roller coasters, tractors, and rainbows—without ever having to leave the comfort of daddy's lap.

RAINBOWS, RAILROADS, AND RHYMES

(Words and lyrics by Rick Burch)

Words to sing and sign:

ALL-DONE, BED, BLANKET, CHAIR, DANCE, FLOWER, KISS, LIGHT-OFF, LOVE/HOLD/HUG, MOMMY, MUSIC/SING, NIGHT-NIGHT, PLAY

Lullaby Bonus Words: **barnyard, baseball, pirate, plane, rainbow, read, rock (in rocking chair), spider, tractor, train/railroad**

Rick Burch, the composer of this song, retrieved it from the archives of his memory only recently after creating it some twelve years ago for his first son, Hayden. His little boy was plagued with colic, which was the result of reflux. Per doctor's orders, his parents rocked him as they read and sang to him for several hours each evening to make sure he digested his evening bottle before lying down in his crib. Rick believed this project was perfect for sharing this story and very special song, as other parents may be in a similar situation with their babies and look to this book for assistance. Rick is happy to report that his baby boy is almost as tall as his dad these days, and has no recollection of why they rocked, read, and sang for hours. What endures for Hayden is that this time spent together with his father was very precious.

Sign suggestions to accompany the song

Verse 1.

When nighttime comes, I take my son,

And we climb into our favorite **chair**.   Sign CHAIR

We *read* about *spiders* and *tractors* and *trains*,   Sign *read* or *spider* or *tractor* or *train*

Flowers and *pirates* and *planes*.   Sign FLOWER or *pirate* or *plane*

And when the *reading* is through,	Sign *read*
Nearly every night, here's what we do.	
We wrap ourselves up in a **blanket**	Sign BLANKET
And I **hold (love)** him in my arms so tight.	Sign LOVE
He lays his head on my shoulder	
As I reach to turn off the light **(light-off)**.	Sign LIGHT-OFF
Yes, we wrap ourselves up in a **blanket**	Sign BLANKET
And *rock* until the day is through **(all-done)**.	Sign *rock* or ALL-DONE
As I put him in **bed**,	Sign BED
I **kiss** him and say,	Sign KISS
"**Good-night**, see you soon."	Sign NIGHT-NIGHT
Verse 2.	
We love to **dance** and laugh and **play**,	Sign DANCE or PLAY
But the best time of day	
Is when we **sing (music)** about *baseball*	Sign MUSIC or *baseball*
and *barnyards* and **bedtime**,	Sign *barnyard* or BED
Rainbows and *railroads (trains)* and rhymes.	Sign *rainbow* or *train*
And when the **singing (music)** is **through**	Sign MUSIC or ALL-DONE
(all-done),	
Nearly every night, here's what we do . . .	
Verse 3.	
And when the *reading* and	Sign *read* or MUSIC
singing (music)	
are **through (all-done)**,	Sign ALL-DONE
Nearly every night, here's what we do . . .	
. . . As I put him in **bed**, he looks up and says:	Sign BED
"**Goodnight, mama**, see you soon."	Sign NIGHT-NIGHT or MOMMY

RAINBOWS, RAILROADS, AND RHYMES

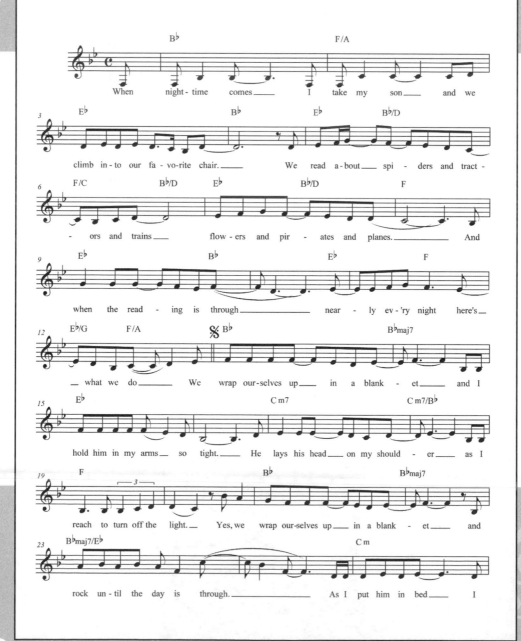

2

kiss him and say___ "Good-night,_____ see you soon."

And when the read-ing and sing - ing are through ___

near - ly ev - 'ry night here's___ what we do_____ We

As I put him in bed,___ he

looks up and says___ "Good - night, ma - ma, see you soon."

NOW I LAY ME DOWN TO SLEEP

(Music by Jennifer Maddox and Anne Meeker Miller/Lyrics by Anne Meeker Miller)

Words to sing and sign:
APPLE, BED/SLEEP, DADDY, DARK, FINE/ALRIGHT, LOVE, MOMMY, PLAY, PRAY, STAR, TREE

Lullaby Bonus Words: **brother, climb, dream, grandma, park, pie, sea, sister, swim, roller coaster**

My grandmother taught me the prayer that begins: "Now I lay me down to sleep." I liked the first phrase of that prayer, but didn't like the part of the prayer that follows: ". . . and if I die before I wake, I pray the Lord my soul to take." I had no interest in dying in my sleep, thank you very much! I wrote this lyric—based loosely on that prayer text—from the point of view of a child and what her conversation with God might sound like. What children want most is to be with the people they love. In the absence of those loved ones, I hope even babies realize they are never alone.

Sign suggestions to accompany the song

Verse 1.
Now I lay me down to **sleep (bed)**.   Sign BED
I **pray**, Dear Lord, my soul to keep.   Sign PRAY
If I *dream* of the *park* in May,   Sign *dream* or *park*
I'll need my **mommy** so we can **play**.   Sign MOMMY or PLAY
And if I *dream*   Sign *dream*
Of an **apple tree**,   Sign APPLE or TREE

My *brother* should be | Sign *brother*
Climbin' with me. | Sign *climb*

Verse 2.

Now I lay me down to **sleep (bed)**. | Sign BED
I **pray**, Dear Lord, my soul to keep. | Sign PRAY
If I *dream* of a day at the *sea*, | Sign *dream* or *sea*
I'd **love** my *grandma* | Sign LOVE or *grandma*
To *swim* with me. | Sign *swim*
And if I *dream* of a sugar *pie*, | Sign *dream* or *pie*
I'd like two pieces—for my *sister* and I. | Sign *sister*
I know it's **dark** | Sign DARK
And it's time for **bed**. | Sign BED
Can't we **love** and **snuggle (love)** instead? | Sign LOVE
I guess that I could use the rest **(bed)**, | Sign BED
But I like to be with you the best.

Verse 3.

Now I lay me down tonight **(bed)**, | Sign BED
I know, Dear Lord, I'll be alright **(fine)** | Sign FINE
And if I *dream* of a *coaster* ride, | Sign *dream* or *roller coaster*
I'll need my **daddy** right by my side. | Sign DADDY
But if it's only me and You,
I know You're with me
The whole **night** through. | Sign NIGHT-NIGHT
Starlight, starbright, | Sign STAR
first **star** I see tonight . . . | Sign STAR
. . . Now I lay you down to **sleep (bed)**. | Sign BED
You are my *dream*, you are my heart **(love)**. | Sign *dream* or LOVE
I **love** you, **baby** mine. | Sign LOVE or BABY
You'll be just **fine**, I'll be here in the morning. | Sign FINE
You are my **love**, you are my life . . . | Sign LOVE

NOW I LAY ME DOWN TO SLEEP

34   Bm   Bm/A   Gmaj7   D/F

by   my side.____   But   if   it's   on - ly

36   F#7   Bm   G/E

me____ and You,____ I____ know You're with

38   G/A   G   D

me   the whole night   through.____

MEALTIME AND BEDTIME SING & SIGN CD INDEX

Singing while you sign is a wonderful way to supply all the repetition and practice your child needs to learn new vocabulary words as he enjoys listening to the music with you. This Sing and Sign CD Index is provided so you can quickly and easily find the signs you are teaching your child in their musical context on the CD.

MEALTIME AND BEDTIME PICTORIAL DICTIONARY

Photographs of all signs taught in this book are compiled alphabetically for you here. These pages can be duplicated so that you can keep a copy in your child's diaper bag or posted on your refrigerator door for quick reference.

AGAIN

ALL-DONE

ALL-GONE

ALRIGHT

APPLE

APPLESAUCE
APPLE plus SPOON

BABY

BAD

BAGEL

BANANA

BARNYARD

BASEBALL

BATH

BATHROOM

BEANS

BEAR

BEAUTIFUL

BED

BIB

BIG

BIRD

BLANKET

BOAT

BOOK

BOWL

BOY

BREAD

BREAKFAST

PLUS

BROTHER

BRUSH-TEETH

BUBBLE

BUG

BUTTERFLY

CAKE

CARROT

CAT

CEREAL

CHAIR

CHANGE

CHEESE

CHOKE

CLIMB

COLD

COMB-HAIR

COOK

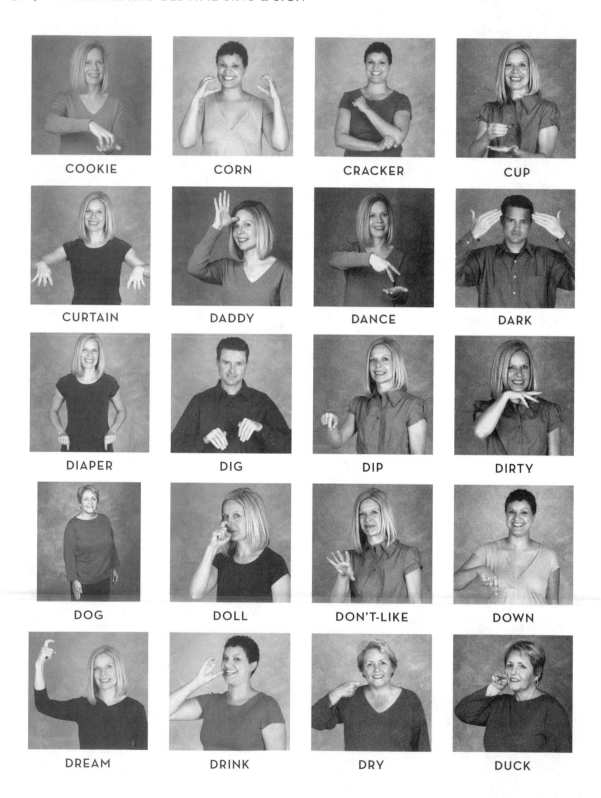

COOKIE	CORN	CRACKER	CUP
CURTAIN	DADDY	DANCE	DARK
DIAPER	DIG	DIP	DIRTY
DOG	DOLL	DON'T-LIKE	DOWN
DREAM	DRINK	DRY	DUCK

EAT	FARM	FAVORITE	FEED
FILL	FINE	FLOWER	FOOD
FORK	FRIEND	FRUIT	FULL
GIRL	GIVE	GO	GOOD
GRANDMA	GRANDPA	GRAPES	HAPPY

HELP	HIDE	HOLD	HOME
HOT	HUG	HUNGRY	ICE CREAM
JUICE	KISS	LIGHT	LIGHT-OFF
LIKE	LITTLE	LOTION	LOVE
LUNCH	MACARONI	MASSAGE	MEALTIME

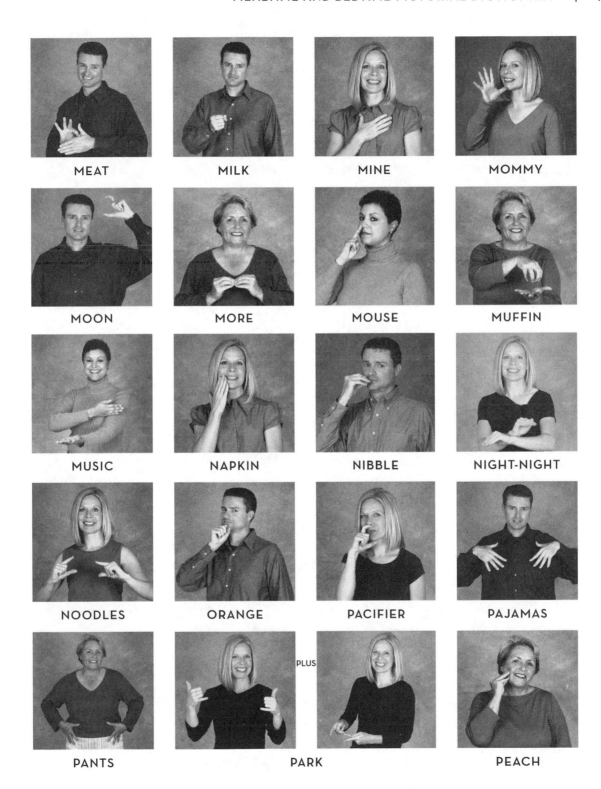

MEAT   MILK   MINE   MOMMY

MOON   MORE   MOUSE   MUFFIN

MUSIC   NAPKIN   NIBBLE   NIGHT-NIGHT

NOODLES   ORANGE   PACIFIER   PAJAMAS

PANTS   PLUS   PARK   PEACH

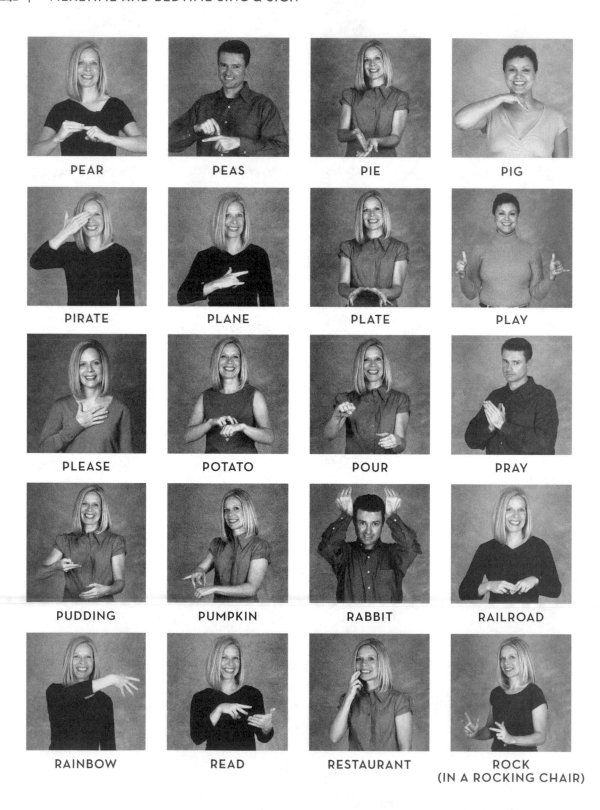

PEAR

PEAS

PIE

PIG

PIRATE

PLANE

PLATE

PLAY

PLEASE

POTATO

POUR

PRAY

PUDDING

PUMPKIN

RABBIT

RAILROAD

RAINBOW

READ

RESTAURANT

ROCK
(IN A ROCKING CHAIR)

ROLLER COASTER	ROOM	ROOSTER	SANDWICH
SCARED	SEA	SHAMPOO	SHEEP
SHIRT	SHOES	SING	
SISTER	SIT	SLEEP	
SMELL	SMILE	SNUGGLE	SOAP

PLUS

SOCKS

SONG

SPAGHETTI

SPIDER

SPLASH

SPOON

STAR

STIR

STOP

STORE

STRAW

SUN

SUPPER

SWEET

SWIM

TABLE

TASTE

THANK YOU

THIRSTY

TIME (FOR BED)

TIRED	TOAST	TOMATO	TOWEL
TOY	TRACTOR	TRAIN	TREE
TUMMY	TURKEY	UP	VEGETABLE
WAFFLE	WAKE	WALK	WANT
WASH	WASH-HAIR	WATER	WET

WHERE

WINDOW

YOGURT

YOU'RE WELCOME

YUCKY

YUMMY

SING AND SIGN—AND READ—WITH PICTURE BOOKS

For your convenience, here is a master list of picture books recommended for infants and toddlers that will help you teach the key signs shared in this program. Copy the list and keep it in your car for trips to your public library. The benefits of early reading with children birth to two are immeasurable; reading provides the foundation for language and literacy by enhancing vocabulary, fluency, and attention span.

ALL-DONE

Dishes All Done by Lucia Monfried (Dutton Children's Books)
Yum, Yum, All Done by Jerry Smath (Grosset and Dunlap)

APPLE

Apples, Apples by Kathleen Weidner Zoehfeld and Christopher Santoro (HarperFestival)
Orange Pear Apple Bear by Emily Gravett (Simon & Schuster Children's Publishing)
Ten Red Apples by Virgina Miller (Candlewick)

BABY

Baby Bear's Chairs by Jane Yolen and Melissa Sweet (Gulliver Books)
The Baby Beebee Bird by Diane Redfield Massie (HarperCollins)

Baby Cakes by Karma Wilson (Little Simon)

Baby Dance by Ann Taylor (HarperFestival)

Baby Duck and the Cozy Blanket by Amy Hest and Jill Barton (Candlewick)

Baby Faces by DK Publishing (DK Publishing)

Baby Faces Board Book: Smile by Roberta Grobel Intrater (Cartwheel)

Baby Food by Margaret Miller (Little Simon)

Bubble Bath Baby by Libby Ellis (Chronicle Books)

Everywhere Babies by Susan Meyers and Marla Frazee (Red Wagon Books)

Hush, Little Baby by Marla Frazee (Voyager Books)

I Kissed the Baby by Mary Murphy (Candlewick Press)

Please, Baby, Please by Spike Lee (Aladdin)

Water Babies Colors by Zena Holloway (Cartwheel)

Where Is Baby's Belly Button? by Karen Katz (Little Simon)

Where Is Baby's Mommy? by Karen Katz (Little Simon)

BAD/YUCKY

Big, Bad Bear by Che Rudko (Reader's Digest)

The Good Little Bad Little Pig by Margaret Wise Brown (Hyperion)

Yummy Yucky by Leslie Patricelli (Candlewick)

BANANA

Goodnight, Gorilla by Peggy Rathmann (Putnam Juvenile)

The Mouse Who Ate Bananas by Keith Faulkner (Orchard)

Who Eats Bananas? by Richard Powell (Treehouse Children's Books Limited)

Wibbly Pig Likes Bananas by Mick Inkpen (Viking Juvenile)

BATH/WASH

Bubble Bath Baby by Libby Ellis (Chronicle Books)

Jack—It's Bath Time! by Elgar (Kingfisher)

Maizy Takes a Bath by Lucy Cousins (Candlewick)

Mrs. Wishy-Washy Board Book by Joy Cowley (Philomel)

BEAR

Baby Bear's Chairs by Jane Yolen and Melissa Sweet (Gulliver Books)

Bear Wants More by Karma Wilson (Simon & Schuster Childrens Books)

A Boy and a Bear by Lori Litel (Specialty Press)

Brown Bear, Brown Bear, What Do You See? by Bill Martin Jr.
   (Henry Holt and Company)

Can't You Sleep, Little Bear? by Martin Waddell and Barbara Firth (Candlewick)

The Chair Where Bear Sits by Lee Wardlaw (Winslow Press)

Jamberry by Bruce Degan (HarperFestival)

Orange Pear Apple Bear by Emily Gravett (Simon & Schuster
   Children's Publishing)

Ten in the Bed: A Counting Book by David Ellwand (Handprint Books)

We're Going on a Bear Hunt by Helen Oxenbury (Little Simon)

Where Are Those Teddy Bears? by Prue Teobalds (Flying Frog Publishing)

Where Does the Brown Bear Go? by Nicki Weiss (Puffin)

BED/SLEEP/REST/TIRED

Bunny Day: Telling Time from Breakfast to Bedtime by Rick Walton (HarperCollins)

Can't You Sleep, Little Bear? by Martin Waddell and Barbara Firth (Candlewick)

Go to Sleep, Daisy by Jane Simmons (Little, Brown)

The Going-to-Bed Book by Sandra Boynton (Little Simon)

So Many Bunnies: A Bedtime ABC and Counting Book by Rick Walton (HarperFestival)

Ten in the Bed: A Counting Book by David Ellwand (Handprint Books)

Time for Bed by Mem Fox and Jane Dyer (Red Wagon Books)

BIRD

The Baby Beebee Bird by Diane Redfield Massie (HarperCollins)

Counting Is for the Birds by Frank Mazzola Jr. (Charlesbridge)

Grumpy Bird by Jeremy Tankard (Scholastic Press)

Hello, Little Bird by Petr Horacek (Walker Books)

I Heard, Said the Bird by Polly Berrien Berends (Puffin Books)

BLANKET

Baby Duck and the Cozy Blanket by Amy Hest and Jill Barton (Candlewick)
Blankie by Leslie Patricelli (Candlewick)
My Blanket by Sandra Magsamen (L,B Kids)
Where's My Fuzzy Blanket? by Noelle Carter (Cartwheel Books)

BOOK

The Best Place to Read by Debbie Bertram and Susan Bloom (Random House)
Bunny's Noisy Book by Margaret Wise Brown (Hyperion)
But Excuse Me That Is My Book by Lauren Child (Tiger Aspect Productions)
I Like Books by Anthony Browne (Candlewick Press)
My Book Box by Will Hillenbrand (Harcourt Brace)

BOY

The Biggest Boy by Kevin Henkes (HarperTrophy)
A Boy and a Bear by Lori Litel (Specialty Press)
A Boy and His Bunny by Sean Bryan (Arcade Publishing)
Goodnight, Monkey Boy by Jarrett J. Krosoczka (Dragonfly Books)
The Puppy Who Wanted a Boy by Jane Thayer (HarperCollins)

BREAD

Blue Bowl Down: An Appalachian Rhyme by C. M. Millen (Candlewick)
Bread Is for Eating by David Gershator (Henry Holt and Company)
Bread, Bread, Bread by Ann Morris (HarperTrophy)

BRUSH-TEETH

Brush Your Teeth Please by Reader's Digest (Reader's Digest)
Brushing My Teeth! by DK Publishing (DK Publishing)
Clarabelle's Teeth by An Vrombaut (Clarion Books)
What Do the Fairies Do with All Those Teeth? by Michel Luppens (Firefly Books)

BUBBLE

Bubble Bath Baby by Libby Ellis (Chronicle Books)
Bubble Bubble by Mercer Mayer (School Specialty Publishing)
Bubbles, Bubbles by Kathi Appelt (HarperFestival)
Clifford Counts Bubbles by Norman Bridwell (Cartwheel)

BUG

Busy Bugs by Mandy Stanley (Kingfisher)
Peek-a-Boo Bugs: A Hide and Seek Book by David A. Carter (Little Simon)
The Icky Bug Counting Book by Jerry Pallotta (Charlesbridge Publishing)
Snappy Little Bugs: See the Bugs Jump, Hop, and Crawl by Dugald Steer
 (Silver Dolphin Books)
Tumble Bumble by Felicia Bond (Harper Trophy)
You're My Little Love Bug by Heidi R. Weimer (Candy Cane Press)

BUTTERFLY

The Butterfly Garden by Sue Harris (Chronicle Books)
Caterpillar Spring, Butterfly Summer by Susan Hood (Reader's Digest)
One Little Butterfly by Wendy Cheyette Lewison (Grosset & Dunlap)
Sheep Don't Count Sheep by Margaret Wise Brown (Margaret K. McElderberry)

CARROT

Carrot in My Pocket by Kitson Flynn (Moon Mountain Publishing)
The Carrot Seed Board Book by Ruth Krauss (HarperFestival)
Carrot Soup by John Segal (Margaret K. McElderry)
Carrots by Inez Snyder (Children's Press)

CAT

Cat Count by Betsy Lewin (Henry Holt and Co.)
Farmer Smart's Fat Cat by James Sage (Chronicle Books)

Find the Kitten by Phil Roxbee Cox (Usborne Publishing)

I Like Cats by Pamela Paparone (North-South)

Mama Cat Has Three Kittens by Denise Fleming (Owlet Paperbacks)

Pat the Cat by Edith Kunhardt Davis (Golden Books)

Sleepy Cat by Inc. Sterling Publishing Company (Inc. Sterling Publishing Company)

CEREAL

The Cheerios Animal Play Book by Lee Wade (Little Simon)

The Cheerios Play Book by Lee Wade (Little Simon)

Oh, David! by David Shannon (Blue Sky Press)

CHAIR

Annie's Chair by Deborah Niland (Walker Books for Young Readers)

Baby Bear's Chairs by Jane Yolen and Melissa Sweet (Gulliver Books)

A Chair for Mother by Vera B. Williams (HarperTrophy)

The Chair Where Bear Sits by Lee Wardlaw (Winslow Press)

Peter's Chair by Ezra Jack Keats (HarperCollins)

CHEESE

The Cheese Chase by Toni Simmons (Beaver's Pond Press, Inc.)

Macaroni and Cheese, Hot Dogs and Peas by Christine Hickson
    (Concordia Publishing House)

Mice Love Cheese (A Guess-Who "Touch-and-Feel" Flap Book) by Richard Powell
    (Barron's Educational Series)

Pop-Up Surprise—Big Cheese by Golden Books (Golden Books)

COMB-HAIR

Comb, Comb: Puppy by Lizzie Nann (Random House Books for Young Readers)

Henry's First Haircut by Dan Yaccarino (Simon Spotlight/Nickelodeon)

I Love My Hair by Natasha Anastasia Tarpley (Little, Brown Young Readers)

I'll Do It Myself by Jirina Marton (Annick Press)

Too Many Curls by Marilyn Kahalewai and Karen Poepoe (Bess Press)

CORN

Corn: A True Book by Elaine Landau (Children's Press)
Farmer Smart's Fat Cat by James Sage (Chronicle Books)
I Like Corn by Robin Pickering (Children's Books)

CRACKER

Animal Crackers: A Delectable Collection of Pictures, Poems, and Lullabies for the Very Young by Jane Dyer (Little, Brown Young Readers)
Baby Food by Margaret Miller (Little Simon)
Pancakes, Crackers, and Pizza: A Book of Shapes by Marjorie Eberts and Margaret Gisler (Children's Press)

DADDY

Daddy and Me by Karen Katz (Little Simon)
Daddy Cuddles by Anne Gutman and Georg Hallensleben (Chronicle Books)
Daddy's Girl by Garrison Keillor (Hyperion)
Daddy's Lullaby by Tony Bradman (Margaret K. McElderry)
Just Like Daddy by Frank Asch (Aladdin)
I Love My Daddy by Sebastien Braun (HarperCollins)
No, I Want Daddy! by Nadine Brun-Cosme (Clarion Books)
Papa, Papa by Jean Marzollo (HarperFestival)
Papa, Please Get the Moon for Me by Eric Carle (Little Simon)
With a Little Help from Daddy by Dan Andreasen (Margaret K. McElderry)

DANCE

Baby Dance by Ann Taylor (HarperFestival)
Barnyard Dance by Sandra Boynton (Workman Publishing Company)
Giraffes Can't Dance by Giles Andreae (Orchard)
Got to Dance by M. C. Helldorfer (Doubleday Books for Young Readers)
Hop, Dance, Jump: Action Words and Fabulous Flaps by Maureen Roffey (Reader's Digest)
Watch Me Dance by Andrea Davis Pinkney (Red Wagon Books)

DARK

Franklin in the Dark by Paulette Bourgeois (Scholastic, Inc.)

Go Away, Dark Night by Liz Curtis Higgs and Nancy Munger (WaterBrook Press)

One Dark Night by Lisa Wheeler (Voyager Books)

The Owl Who Was Afraid of the Dark by Jill Tomlinson (Egmont Books, Limited)

DIG

Bob's Big Dig by Bendix Anderson (Golden Books)

Dig Dig Digging by Margaret Mayo (Henry Holt and Company)

Dig, Drill, Dump, Fill by Tana Hoben (Mulberry Books)

Dig In by Dana Meachen Rau (Benchmark Books)

A Hole Is to Dig by Ruth Krauss (HarperCollins)

DOG

Bark, George by Jules Feiffer (Laura Geringer)

Dog by Matthew Van Fleet (Simon & Schuster / Paula Wiseman Books)

Doggies: A Counting and Barking Book by Sandra Boynton (Little Simon)

Give the Dog a Bone by S. Kellogg (SeaStar)

Go, Dog. Go! (Cloth Book) by P. D. Eastman (Random House Books for Young Readers)

That's Not My Puppy: Its Coat Is Too Hairy by Fiona Watt (Usborne Books)

The Puppy Who Wanted a Boy by Jane Thayer (HarperCollins)

DOWN

All Fall Down by Helen Oxenbury (Little Simon)

Deep Down Underground by Olivier Dunrea (Aladdin)

Down by the Bay by Raffi (Crown Books for Young Readers)

Down by the Station by Will Hillenbrand (Voyager Books)

Fletcher and the Falling Leaves by Julia Rawlinson (Greenwillow)

Sun Up, Sun Down by Gail Gibbons (Voyager)

Up, Down, and Around by Katherine Ayres (Candlewick)

DRINK

Deer at the Brook by Jim Arnosky (Mulberry Pr)

Llama Llama, Red Pajama by Anna Dewdney (Viking Juvenile)

Night Tree by Eve Bunting (Harcourt)

While the Moon Shines Bright by Jeanne Whitehouse Peterson (HarperCollins)

DRY

Better Not Get Wet, Jesse Bear by Nancy White Carstrom (Aladdin)

The Duck Who Loved Puddles by Michael J. Peliowski (Troll Communications)

Theodore by Edward Ormondroud (Parnassus Press)

DUCK

Across the Stream by Mira Ginsburg & Daniil Kharms (HarperTrophy)

Baby Duck and the Cozy Blanket by Amy Hest and Jill Barton (Candlewick)

Five Little Ducks by Raffi (Crown Books for Young Readers)

Fuzzy Yellow Ducklings by Matthew Van Pleet (Dial)

Have You Seen My Duckling? by Nancy Tafuri (HarperTrophy)

No More Diapers for Ducky! by Bernette Ford (Boxer Books)

EAT/FOOD/NIBBLE

Benji Bean Sprout Doesn't Eat Meat by Sarah Rudy (SK Publishing)

Bread Is for Eating by David Gershator (Henry Holt and Company)

Bronto Eats Meat by Peter Maloney (Dial)

Eat Up, Gemma by Sarah Hayes (HarperTrophy)

Eat Your Peas, Ivy Louise by Leo Landry (Houghton Mifflin)

Eating the Alphabet by Lois Ehlert (Red Wagon)

Everybody Eats Rice by Norah Dooley (Houghton Mifflin Company)

The Giant Sandwich by Seth M. Agnew (Houghton Mifflin)

How Do Dinosaurs Eat Their Food? by Jane Yolen (HarperCollins Children)

I Will Never Not Ever Eat a Tomato by Lauren Child (Candlewick)

It's the Bear by Jez Alborough (Candlewick)

Like Butter on Pancakes by Jonathon London (Puffin)

Who Eats Bananas? by Richard Powell (Treehouse Children's Books Limited)

FILL

Baby Einstein: Violet's House: A Giant Touch-and-Feel Book by Julie Aigner-Clark (Baby Einstein Co)

Dig, Drill, Dump, Fill by Tana Hoben (Mulberry Books)

Fill It Up: All About Service Stations by Gail Gibbons (HarperCollins Publishers)

FINE/ALRIGHT

One Fine Day by Molly Bang (Greenwillow Books)

One Fine Day (Stories to Go) by Nonny Hogrogian (Aladdin)

Spending Time with Big Jake (Jay Jay the Jet Plane) by Grace Maxfield (Price Stern Sloan)

FLOWER

Bees Love Flowers (Touch & Feel Flap Books) by Richard Powell (Treehouse Children's Books Ltd)

Flower Garden by Eve Bunting (Voyager Books)

Flower Girl by Laura Godwin (Hyperion)

Hurray for Spring! by Patricia Hubbell (NorthWord Books for Young Readers)

Song of the Flowers by Takayo Noda (Dial)

What Does Bunny See?: A Book of Colors and Flowers by Linda Sue Park (Clarion Books)

FRIEND

Do You Want to Be My Friend? by Eric Carle (Philomel)

A Friend Is Someone Who Likes You by Joan Walsh Anglund (Harcourt Children's Books)

Harvey the Gardener by Lars Klinting (Kingfisher)

My Friend Bear by Jex Alborough (Candlewick)

Where Are Maisy's Friends? by Lucy Cousins (Walker Books Ltd)

FRUIT

A Book of Fruit by Barbara Hirsch Lember (Ticknor & Fields)

Each Peach Pear Plum by Janet and Allan Ahlberg (Viking Juvenile)

Growing Colors by Bruce McMillan (HarperTrophy)

The Very Hungry Caterpillar by Eric Carle (Black Butterfly Children's Books)

GIRL

A Beautiful Girl by Amy Schwartz (Roaring Brook Press)

Daddy's Girl by Garrison Keillor (Hyperion)

Flower Girl by Laura Godwin (Hyperion)

The Listening Walk by Paul Showers (HarperTrophy)

Tummy Girl by Roseanne Thong (Henry Holt and Co.)

GIVE

Biscuit Gives a Gift by Alyssa Satin Capucilli (HarperFestival)

Give the Dog a Bone by S. Kellogg (SeaStar)

I'll Give You Kisses by Diane Paterson (Dial)

If You Give a Moose a Muffin by Laura Numeroff (Laura Geringer)

GO

Cars and Trucks and Things That Go by Richard Scarry (Golden Books)

Go, Dog. Go! (Cloth Book) by P. D. Eastman (Random House Books for Young Readers)

Go Away, Dark Night by Liz Curtis Higgs and Nancy Munger (WaterBrook Press)

Go to Sleep, Daisy by Jane Simmons (Little, Brown)

Ready, Set, Go! (Board Book) by Nina Laden (Chronicle Books)

Red, Stop! Green, Go! by P. D. Eastman (Random House)

Off We Go! by Jane Yolen (Little, Brown Young Readers)

Where Does the Brown Bear Go? by Nicki Weiss (Puffin)

GOOD/YUMMY

The Good Little Bad Little Pig by Margaret Wise Brown (Hyperion)

Yum, Yum, All Done by Jerry Smath (Grosset and Dunlap)

Yum, Yum, Yummy! by Martin Waddell (Candlewick)

Yummy Chocolate Bunny by Jocelyn Jamison (Price Stern Sloan)

Yummy Yucky by Leslie Patricelli (Candlewick)

Yummy Yummy, Food for My Tummy! by Sam Lloyd (Little Tiger Press)

GRAPES

Eat Up, Gemma by Sarah Hayes (HarperTrophy)

My Grapes by Megan McGrath (Scholastic)

HAPPY

The Happy Day by Ruth Krauss (HarperTrophy)

If You're Happy and You Know It by Jane Cabrera (Holiday House)

If You're Happy and You Know It, Clap Your Hands by David Carter (Cartwheel)

Wibbly Pig Is Happy by Mick Inkpen (Viking Juvenile)

HELP

One Duck Stuck by Phyllis Root (Candlewick)

The Shelf Elf Helps Out by Jackie Mims Hopkins (Upstart Books)

Spot Helps Out by Eric Hill (Putnam Juvenile)

With a Little Help from Daddy by Dan Andreasen (Margaret K. McElderry)

HIDE

Animal Hide-and-Seek (Touchy Feely Flap Book) by Jenny Tyler (Usborne Books)

Five Little Monkeys Play Hide-and-Seek by Eileen Christelow (Clarion books)

Hide and Seek (Minerva Louise Board Book) by Janet Morgan Stoeke (Dutton Juvenile)

McDuff's Hide-and-Seek: Lift the Flap/Pull the Tab Book by Rosemary Wells (Hyperion)

Peek-A-Boo! by Janet Ahlberg (Viking Juvenile)

Peek-a-Boo Bugs: A Hide and Seek Book by David A. Carter (Little Simon)

HOME

Mama Always Comes Home by Karma Wilson (HarperTrophy)

An Octopus Followed Me Home by Dan Yaccarino (Puffin)

Owl at Home by Arnold Lobel (Scholastic)

HUNGRY

Bear Snores On by Karma Wilson (Simon & Schuster Childrens Books)

The Little Mouse, the Red Ripe Strawberry, and the Big Hungry Bear by Don & Audrey Wood (Masters Press)

Lunch by Denise Fleming (Henry Holt and Co.)

One Hungry Monster: A Counting Book in Rhyme by Susan Heyboer O'Keefe (Joy Street Books)

The Very Hungry Caterpillar by Eric Carle (Black Butterfly Children's Books)

KISS

How Many Kisses Do You Want Tonight? by Varsha Bajaj (Little, Brown Young Readers)

I Kissed the Baby by Mary Murphy (Candlewick Press)

If Kisses Were Colors by Janet Lawler (Dial)

Kiss Kiss! by Margaret Wild (Simon & Schuster Children's Publishing)

Won't You Be My Kissaroo? by Joanne Ryder (Gulliver Books)

LIGHT-OFF

Eli's Night Light by Liz Rosenberg (Orchard)

One Light One Sun by Raffi (Dragonfly Books)

This Little Light of Mine by Public Domain (Simon & Schuster Children's Publishing)

This Little Light of Mine by Raffi (Knopf Books for Young Readers)

LOVE/HOLD/HUG/SNUGGLE

Bees Love Flowers (Touch & Feel Flap Books) by Richard Powell (Treehouse Children's Books Ltd)

Carry Me! by Rosemary Wells (Little Brown & Co)

Do You Still Love Me? by Charlotte Middleton (Candlewick)

The Duck Who Loved Puddles by Michael J. Peliowski (Troll Communications)

Guess How Much I Love You by Sam McBratney (Walker Books Ltd)

Hug by Jez Alborough (Candlewick)

I Love Animals by Flora McDonnell (Candlewick)

I Love It When You Smile by Sam Bratney (HarperCollins)

I Love My Daddy by Sebastien Braun (HarperCollins)

I Love My Hair by Natasha Anastasia Tarpley (Little, Brown Young Readers)

I Love You Sun / I Love You Moon by Karen Pandell (Putnam Juvenile)

Mice Love Cheese (A Guess-Who "Touch-and-Feel" Flap Book) by Richard Powell (Barron's Educational Series)

"More, More, More" Said the Baby: Three Love Stories by Vera B. Williams (HarperTrophy)

You're My Little Love Bug by Heidi R. Weimer (Candy Cane Press)

MEAT

Benji Bean Sprout Doesn't Eat Meat by Sarah Rudy (SK Publishing)

Bronto Eats Meat by Peter Maloney (Dial)

Chicken Soup with Rice by Maurice Sendak (Scholastic)

Green Eggs and Ham by Dr. Seuss (Random House Books for Young Readers)

Macaroni and Cheese, Hot Dogs and Peas by Christine Hickson (Concordia Publishing House)

On Top of Spaghetti by Paul Brett Johnson (Scholastic Press)

MILK

It Looked Like Spilt Milk by Charles G. Shaw (HarperTrophy)

The Milk Makers by Gail Gibbons (Aladdin)

The Wee Little Woman by Bryon Barton (HarperCollins)

MOMMY

Are You My Mother? by P. D. Eastman (Random House Books for Young Readers)

Daisy Is a Mommy by Lisa Kopper (Dutton Juvenile)

Is Your Mama a Llama? by Deborah Guarino (Scholastic Press)

Mommy Mine by Tim Warnes (HarperCollins)

Where Is Baby's Mommy? by Karen Katz (Little Simon)

Where's My Mommy? by Jo Brown (Tiger Tales)

Will You Carry Me? by Heleen Van Rossum (Kane/Miller Book Publishers)

MOON

Goodnight Sun, Hello Moon by Reader's Digest (Reader's Digest)

I Love You Sun / I Love You Moon by Karen Pandell (Putnam Juvenile)

The Moon by Robert Stevenson (Farrar, Straus and Giroux)

The Moon Jumpers by Janice May Udry (Michael Di Capua Books)

Papa, Please Get the Moon for Me by Eric Carle (Little Simon)

Where Does the Brown Bear Go? by Nicki Weiss (Puffin)

While the Moon Shines Bright by Jeanne Whitehouse Peterson (HarperCollins)

MORE

Bear Wants More by Karma Wilson (Simon & Schuster Childrens Books)

"More, More, More" Said the Baby: Three Love Stories by Vera B. Williams (HarperTrophy)

No More Diapers for Ducky! by Bernette Ford (Boxer Books)

One More Sheep by Mij Kelly (Peachtree Publishers)

MOUSE

Inside Mouse, Outside Mouse by Lindsay Barrett (HarperTrophy)

The Little Mouse, the Red Ripe Strawberry, and the Big Hungry Bear by Don & Audrey Wood (Masters Press)

Miss Mouse's Day by Jan Ormerod (HarperCollins Publishers)

Mouse Mess by Linnea Asplind Riley (Blue Sky Press)

Mouse Paint by Ellen Stoll Walsh (Red Wagon Books)

The Mouse Who Ate Bananas by Keith Faulkner (Orchard)

Off We Go! by Jane Yolen (Little, Brown Young Readers)

MUFFIN

If You Give a Moose a Muffin by Laura Numeroff (Laura Geringer)

The Musical Muffin Man (Rub-a-Dub Books) by Irena Romendik (Straight Edge Press)

MUSIC/SING/SONG

Grateful: A Song of Giving Thanks by John Bucchino (HarperTrophy)

I Make Music by Eloise Greenfield (Black Butterfly Children's Books)

The Musical Muffin Man (Rub-a-Dub Books) by Irena Romendik
(Straight Edge Press)

Philadelphia Chickens by Sandra Boynton (Workman Publishing Company)

Rhinoceros Tap by Sandra Boynton (Workman Publishing Company)

Sing-Along Song by JoAnn Early Macken (Viking Juvenile)

Song of the Flowers by Takayo Noda (Dial)

Train Song by Harriet Ziefert (Orchard)

NIGHT-NIGHT

A Child's Good Night Prayer by Grace Maccarone (Scholastic Inc.)

Good Night, Fairies by Kathleen Hague (Chronicle Books)

Good Night, God Bless by Susan Heyboer O'Keefe (Henry Holt and Co.)

Good Night, Gorilla by Peggy Rathmann (Putnam Juvenile)

Good Night, Mr. Night by Dan Yaccarino (Voyager Books)

Goodnight Sun, Hello Moon by Reader's Digest (Reader's Digest)

Goodnight, Goodnight, Sleepyhead by Ruth Krauss (HarperCollins)

I'll See You in the Morning by Mike Jolley (Chronicle Books)

Night Tree by Eve Bunting (Harcourt)

Nighty Night! by Margaret Wild (Peachtree Publishers)

NOODLES/MACARONI

Everybody Brings Noodles by Norah Dooley (Carolrhoda Books)

I Like Pasta by Jennifer Julius (Tandem)

Macaroni and Cheese, Hot Dogs and Peas by Christine Hickson
(Concordia Publishing House)

Sometimes I Wonder If Poodles Like Noodles by Laura Numeroff (Aladdin)

ORANGE

Autumn Orange by Christianne C. Jones (Picture Window Books)

Orange in my World by Joanne Winne (Children's Press)

Orange Pear Apple Bear by Emily Gravett (Simon & Schuster Children's Publishing)

PAJAMAS

Llama Llama, Red Pajama by Anna Dewdney (Viking Juvenile)

Llamas in Pajamas by Teddy Slater (Sterling)

Pajama Time by Sandra Boynton (Workman Publishing Company)

PANTS

If Elephants Wore Pants by Henriette Barkow (Sterling)

Jesse Bear, What Will You Wear? by Nancy White Carlstrom (Aladdin)

Pants by Giles Andreae (David Fickling Books)

PEACH

Each Peach Pear Plum by Janet and Allan Ahlberg (Viking Juvenile)

Eating the Alphabet by Lois Ehlert (Red Wagon)

P Is for Peach: A Georgia Alphabet by Carol Crane (Sleeping Bear Press)

Pop-Up Surprise—Fuzzy Peach by Golden Books (Golden Books)

PEAR

Each Peach Pear Plum by Janet and Allan Ahlberg (Viking Juvenile)

Eating the Alphabet by Lois Ehlert (Red Wagon)

Orange Pear Apple Bear by Emily Gravett (Simon & Schuster Children's Publishing)

PEAS

Eat Your Peas, Ivy Louise by Leo Landry (Houghton Mifflin)

Little Pea by Amy Krouse Rosenthal (Chronicle Books)

Macaroni and Cheese, Hot Dogs and Peas by Christine Hickson
    (Concordia Publishing House)
Mabel O'Leary Put Peas in Her Ear-y by Mary Delaney
    (Little, Brown Young Readers)
Muncha! Muncha! Muncha! by Candace Fleming (Simon & Schuster)

PIG

Barnyard Banter by Denise Fleming (Henry Holt and Co.)
Piggies by Audrey Wood (Red Wagon Books)
Wibbly Pig Is Happy by Mick Inkpen (Vicking Juvenile)
Wibbly Pig Likes Bananas by Mick Inkpen (Viking Juvenile)

PLAY/TOY

Biscuit Wants to Play by Alyssa Satin Capucilli (HarperFestival)
The Cheerios Animal Play Book by Lee Wade (Little Simon)
The Cheerios Play Book by Lee Wade (Little Simon)
Five Little Monkeys Play Hide-and-Seek by Eileen Christelow (Clarion books)
Maisy's Big Flap Book by Lucy Cousins (Candlewick)
Mouse Paint by Ellen Stoll Walsh (Red Wagon Books)
Peek-a-Boo! by Janet Ahlberg (Viking Juvenile)
You're Just What I Need by Ruth Krauss (HarperTrophy)

PLEASE

Brush Your Teeth Please by Reader's Digest (Reader's Digest)
Papa, Please Get the Moon for Me by Eric Carle (Little Simon)
Please, Baby, Please by Spike Lee (Aladdin)
Please, Puppy, Please by Spike Lee (Aladdin)
Say "Please:" A Book about Manners by Catherine Lucas
    (Simon Spotlight/Nickelodeon)
What's the Magic Word? by Kelly Dipucchio (HarperCollins)

POTATO

The Enormous Potato by Aubry Davis (Kids Can Press Ltd.)

How Are You Peeling? Foods with Moods by Saxton Freymann and Joost Elffers (Scholastic Inc.)

One Potato: A Counting Book of Potato Prints by Diana Pomeroy (Voyager)

PRAY

A Child's Good Night Prayer by Grace Maccarone (Scholastic Inc.)

Good Night, God Bless by Susan Heyboer O'Keefe (Henry Holt and Co.)

Grateful: A Song of Giving Thanks by John Bucchino (HarperTrophy)

Mortimer's Christmas Manger by Karma Wilson (Margaret K. McElderry)

RABBIT

A Boy and His Bunny by Sean Bryan (Arcade Publishing)

Bunny Day: Telling Time from Breakfast to Bedtime by Rick Walton (HarperCollins)

Knuffle Bunny by Mo Willems (Walker Books Ltd.)

Pat the Bunny by Dorothy Kunhardt (Golden Books)

So Many Bunnies: A Bedtime ABC and Counting Book by Rick Walton (HarperFestival)

What Does Bunny See?: A Book of Colors and Flowers by Linda Sue Park (Clarion Books)

Yummy Chocolate Bunny by Jocelyn Jamison (Price Stern Sloan)

ROOSTER

Farmer Dale's Red Pickup Truck by Lisa Wheeler (Voyager Books)

Hurry! Hurry! by Eve Bunting (Harcourt Children's Books)

Rooster Can't Cock-a-Doodle-Doo by Karen Rostoker-Gruber (Puffin)

SHEEP

Brown Bear, Brown Bear, What Do You See? by Bill Martin Jr. (Henry Holt and Company)

One More Sheep by Mij Kelly (Peachtree Publishers)

Sheep Asleep by Gloria L. Rothstein (HarperCollins)

Sheep Don't Count Sheep by Margaret Wise Brown (Margaret K. McElderberry)

Sheep in a Jeep by Nancy Shaw (Houghton Mifflin)

When Sheep Sleep by Laura Numeroff (Abrams Books for Young Readers)

Where Is the Green Sheep? by Mem Fox (Chrysalis Children's Books)

Who Will Tuck Me in Tonight? by Carol Roth (North-South)

SHIRT

Ella Sarah Gets Dressed by Margaret Chodos-Irvine (Harcourt Children's Books)

Max's Dragon Shirt by Rosemary Wells (Puffin)

Where Is Baby's Belly Button? by Karen Katz (Little Simon)

SHOES

All about Alfie by Shirley Hughes (HarperCollins Publishers)

Gossie and Gertie by Olivier Dunrea (Houghton Mifflin)

Whose Shoes? by Anna Grossnickle Hines (Harcourt Children's Books)

SMILE

Baby Faces Board Book: Smile by Roberta Grobel Intrater (Cartwheel)

I Love It When You Smile by Sam Bratney (HarperCollins)

Smile a Lot! by Nancy L. Carlson (Carolrhoda Books)

SOAP

The Biggest Soap by Carole Lexa Shafer (Farrar, Straus and Giroux)

My World by Margaret Wise Brown (HarperTrophy)

Where Is Slippery Soap? by Buster Yablonsky (Tandem)

SOCKS

Caps, Hats, Socks, and Mittens by Louise W. Borden (Scholastic)

Fox in Socks (Dr. Seuss Board Book) by Dr. Suess (Picture Lions)

Lucky Socks by Carrie Weston (Gullane Children's Books)

SPLASH

Duckie's Splash by Frances Barry (Candlewick)

Splash! by Ann Jonas (HarperTrophy)

Splash! by Flora McDonnell (Walker Books Ltd)

STAR

Good Night, Fairies by Kathleen Hague (Chronicle Books)

How to Catch a Star by Oliver Jeffers (HarperCollins Children's Books)

The Stars Will Still Shine by Cynthia Rylant (HarperCollins)

Twinkle, Twinkle Little Star by Iza Trapani (Charlesbridge Publishing)

STOP

Red, Stop! Green, Go! by P. D. Eastman (Random House)

Stop and Go, Maisy! by Lucy Cousins (Candlewick)

Stop, Train, Stop! (A Thomas the Tank Engine Story) by W. Rev. Awdry (Random House)

STORE

A Chair for Mother by Vera B. Williams (HarperTrophy)

Move Over, Rover! by Karen Beaumont (Harcourt Children's Books)

Sam's Busy Day by Yvew Got (Chronicle Books)

SUN

Goodnight Sun, Hello Moon by Reader's Digest (Reader's Digest)

Hello, Sun! by Dayle Ann Dodds (Dial)

I Love You Sun / I Love You Moon by Karen Pandell (Putnam Juvenile)

One Light One Sun by Raffi (Dragonfly Books)

Sun Up, Sun Down by Gail Gibbons (Voyager)

You Are My Sunshine by Steve Metzger (Scholastic Inc.)

TOMATO

Growing Vegetable Soup by Lois Ehlert (Harcourt/Voyager Books)

I Will Never Not Ever Eat a Tomato by Lauren Child (Candlewick)

The Vegetable Alphabet by Jerry Pallotta (Charlesbridge Publishing)

TREE

Climb the Family Tree, Jess Bear! by Nancy White Carlstrom (Simon & Schuster Children's Publishing)

Five Little Monkeys Sitting in a Tree by Eileen Christelow (Clarion Books)

Kipper's Tree House (Lift the Flap) by Mick Inkpen (Red Wagon Books)

Leo's Tree by Debora Pearson (Annick Press)

Night Tree by Eve Bunting (Harcourt)

Okomi: Climbs a Tree by Helen Dorman (Dawn Publications)

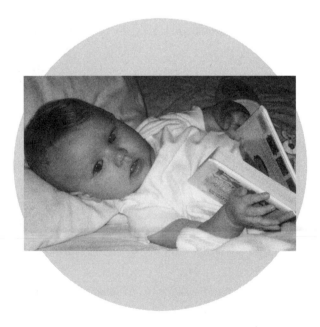

TUMMY

A, B, C, D, Tummy, Toes, Hands, Knees by B. G. Hennessy (Puffin)

Tummy Girl by Roseanne Thong (Henry Holt and Co.)

Yum Tummy Tickly by Karen Baicker (Handprint)

Yummy Yummy, Food for My Tummy! by Sam Lloyd (Little Tiger Press)

UP

Giddy-up! Let's Ride by Flora McDonnell (New Line Books)

Sun Up, Sun Down by Gail Gibbons (Voyager)

The Wheels on the Bus by Paul O. Zelinsky (Dutton Juvenile)

Up, Down, and Around by Katherine Ayres (Candlewick)

Wheels on the Bus by Raffi (Crown Books for Young Readers)

WALK

I Went Walking by Sue Williams (Red Wagon Books)

The Listening Walk by Paul Showers (HarperTrophy)

Rosie's Walk by Pat Hutchins (Aladdin)

WANT

Bear Wants More by Karma Wilson (Simon & Schuster Childrens Books)

Biscuit Wants to Play by Alyssa Satin Capucilli (HarperFestival)

Do You Want to Be My Friend? by Eric Carle (Philomel)

How Many Kisses Do You Want Tonight? by Varsha Bajaj
    (Little, Brown Young Readers)

The Little Red Hen by Paul Galdone (Clarion Books)

No, I Want Daddy! by Nadine Brun-Cosme (Clarion Books)

The Puppy Who Wanted a Boy by Jane Thayer (HarperCollins)

WATER

Water Babies Colors by Zena Holloway (Cartwheel)

The Water Hole by Graeme Base (Harry N. Abrams)

Water, Water by Eloise Greenfield (HarperFestival)

WHERE

The Chair Where Bear Sits by Lee Wardlaw (Winslow Press)

Duck's Key: Where Can It Be? by Jez Alborough (Kane/Miller Book Publishers)

Where Are Maisy's Friends? by Lucy Cousins (Walker Books Ltd)

Where Are Those Teddy Bears? by Prue Teobalds (Flying Frog Publishing)

Where Does the Brown Bear Go? by Nicki Weiss (Puffin)

Where Is Baby's Belly Button? by Karen Katz (Little Simon)

Where Is Baby's Mommy? by Karen Katz (Little Simon)

Where Is Slippery Soap? by Buster Yablonsky (Tandem)

Where Is the Green Sheep? by Mem Fox (Chrysalis Children's Books)

Where's My Fuzzy Blanket? by Noelle Carter (Cartwheel Books)

Where's My Mommy? by Jo Brown (Tiger Tales)

REFERENCES AND RESOURCES

♪ Sign Language and Child Development

Acredolo, Linda, and Susan Goodwyn. *Baby Minds.* New York: Bantam Books, 2000.

_____. *Baby Signs.* Chicago: Contemporary Books, 1996.

Adamek, Mary S. and Alice-Ann Darrow. *Music in Special Education.* Silver Springs, Maryland. The American Music Therapy Association, Inc., 2005.

Alcock, Katie. "The Development of Oral Motor Control and Language." *Down Syndrome Research and Practice* (2006), 1–8.

Apel, Ken, and Julie Masterson. *Beyond Baby Talk: From Sounds to Sentences, a Parent's Guide to Language Development.* Roseville: Prima Publishing, 2001.

Armstrong, Thomas. *In Their Own Way: Discovering and Encouraging Your Child's Multiple Intelligences.* New York: Tarcher, 2000.

Bahan, Ben, and Joe Dannis. *Signs for Me: Basic Sign Vocabulary for Children, Parents, and Teachers.* San Diego, CA: Dawn Sign Press, 1990.

Bailey, Becky. *I Love You Rituals.* New York: Harper Paperbacks, 2000.

Baker, Pamela, and Patricia B. Bellen Gillen. *My First Book of Sign.* Washington, DC: Gallaudet University Press, 2002.

Blakemore, Caroline J. and Barbara Weston Ramirez. *Baby Read-Aloud Basics: Fun and Interactive Ways to Help Your Little One Discover the World of Words.* New York: Amacom, 2006.

Church, Ellen Booth. "The Importance of Pretend Play." *Scholastic.* http://content.scholastic .com/browse/article.jsp?id=10175.

Cohen, Lawrence J. *Playful Parenting: A Bold New Way to Nurture.* New York: Ballantine, 2001.

Conkling, Winifred. *Smart-Wiring Your Baby's Brain: What You Can Do to Stimulate Your Child during the Critical First Three Years.* New York: HarperCollins, 2001.

Crain, William. *Reclaiming Childhood.* New York: Henry Holt, 2003.

Daniels, Marilyn. *Dancing with Words: Signing for Hearing Children's Literacy.* Westport, CT: Bergin and Garvey, 2001.

Garcia, Joseph. *Sign with Your Baby: How to Communicate with Infants before They Can Speak.* Seattle, WA: Northlight Communications, 1999.

Gerber, Magda, and Allison Johnson. *Your Self-Confident Baby: How to Encourage Your Child's Natural Abilities from the Very Start.* Darby, PA: Diane Publishing Company, 1998.

Golinkoff, Roberta M., and Kathy Hirsh-Pasek. *How Babies Talk: The Magic and Mystery of Language in the First Three Years of Life.* New York: Penguin, 1999.

Goodwyn, Susan, and Linda Acredolo, "Encouraging Symbolic Gestures: Effects on the Relationship between Gesture and Speech." In J. Iverson and S. Goldin-Meadows, eds. *The Nature and Functions of Gesture in Children's Communication* (San Francisco: Jossey-Bass, 1998), 61–73.

————, and Catherine A. Brown. "Impact of Symbolic Gesturing on Early Language Development." In *Journal of Nonverbal Behavior* (Summer 2000): 24–2.

Gopnik, Alison, Andrew N. Meltoff, and Patricia Kuhl. *The Scientist in the Crib: What Early Learning Tells Us about the Mind.* New York: HarperCollins, 1999.

Hafer, Jan, Robert Wilson, and Paul Setzer. *Come Sign with Us: Sign Language Activities for Children.* Washington, DC: Gallaudet University Press, 2002.

Hanessian, Lu. *Let the Baby Drive: Navigating the Road of New Motherhood.* New York: St. Martin's, 2004.

Hart, Betty, and Todd Risley. *Meaningful Differences in the Everyday Lives of Children.* Baltimore: Brookes Publishing, 1995.

Karp, Harvey. *The Happiest Baby on the Block: The New Way to Calm Crying and Help Your Baby Sleep Longer.* New York: Bantam, 2002.

————, and Paula Spencer. *The Happiest Toddler on the Block: The New Way to Stop the Daily Battle of Wills and Raise a Secure and Well-Behaved One- to Four-Year-Old.* New York: Bantam, 2005.

"Kids Who Blow Bubbles Find Language Is Child's Play." *Science Daily,* June 28, 2006. http://www.scienceddaily.com/releases/2006/06/060628095606.htm.

McGuinness, Diane. *Growing a Reader from Birth: Your Child's Path from Language to Literacy.* New York: W. W. Norton, 2004.

Miller, Anne Meeker. *Baby Sing & Sign: Communicate Early with Your Baby—Learning Signs the Fun Way through Music and Play.* New York: Marlowe and Company, 2006.

————. *Toddler Sing & Sign: Improve Your Child's Vocabulary and Verbal Skills the Fun Way—Through Music and Play.* New York: Marlowe and Company, 2007.

Owens, Robert E., and Leah Feldon. *Help Your Baby Talk: Introducing the Shared Communication Method to Jump Start Language and Have a Smarter and Happier Baby.* New York: Berkley Publishing Group, 2004.

"Parents' Instinctive Use of Isolated Words May Help Babies Learn Language." *Science Daily,* February 28, 2001. http://www.sciencedaily.com/releases/2001/02/010223081658.htm.

Pica, Rae. *A Running Start: How Play, Physical Activity, and Free Time Create a Successful Child.* New York: Marlowe and Company, 2007.

Pruden, S. M., Kathy Hirsh-Pasek, and E. A. Hennen. "The Birth of Words: Ten-Month-Olds Learn Words through Perceptual Salience." In *Society for Research in Child Development* (March 22, 2006): 77–2.

Rimm, Sylvia. *How to Parent So Children Will Learn.* Watertown, WI: Apple, 1990.

"Rockabye Baby: Research Shows Gentle Singing Soothes Sick Infants." *Science Daily,* February 14, 2006. http://www.sciencedaily.com/releases/2006/02/060213102134.htm.

Rogers, Fred. *The Giving Box: Create a Tradition of Giving with Your Children.* Philadelphia, PA: Running Press Book Publishers, 2000.

_____. *The World According to Mister Rogers: Important Things to Remember.* New York: Hyperion, 2003.

Rosenfeld, Alvin, and Nicole Wise. *Hyper-Parenting: Are You Hurting Your Child by Trying Too Hard?* New York: St. Martin's, 2000.

Sandford, Carolyn. "Using 'Rare' Words at Mealtimes Can Enlarge Children's Vocabulary." *Washington University (St. Louis) Archives.* http://record.wust.edu/archive/1995/09-28-95/4234.html.

Schaefer, Charles E., and Theresa Foy DiGeronimo. *Ages and Stages: A Parent's Guide to Normal Childhood Development.* New York: John Wiley, 2000.

Schank, Roger. *Coloring Outside the Lines: Raising a Smarter Kid by Breaking All the Rules.* New York: HarperCollins, 2000.

Schwartz, Sue, and Joan Heller Miller. *The New Language of Toys: Teaching Communication Skills to Children with Special Needs, A Guide for Parents and Teachers.* Bethesda, MD: Woodbine House, 2004.

Shore, Rima. *What Kids Need.* Boston: Beacon Press, 2002.

Silberg, Jackie. *125 Brain Games for Babies: Simple Games to Promote Early Brain Development.* Beltsville, MD: Gryphon House, 2006.

_____, Pamela Byrne Schiller and Deborah C. Wright. *The Complete book of Rhymes, Songs, Poems, Fingerplays, and Chants: Over 700 Selections.* Beltsville, MD: Gryphon House, 2006.

Slier, Debby. *Animal Signs.* Washington, DC: Gallaudet University Press, 2002.

Stewart, David. *American Sign Language the Easy Way.* Hauppauge, NY: Barron's Educational Series, 1998.

Stipek, Deborah, and Kathy Seal. *Motivated Minds: Raising Children to Love Learning.* New York: Owl Books, 2001.

Straub, Susan, and K. J. Dell'Antonia. *Reading with Babies, Toddlers, and Twos.* Naperville, IL: Sourcebooks, 2006.

Trelease, Jim. *The Read-Aloud Handbook,* 6th ed. New York: Penguin, 2006.

Warburton, Karyn. *Baby Sign Language for Hearing Babies.* New York: Penguin, 2006.

Ward, Sally. *Baby Talk: Strengthen Your Child's Ability to Listen, Understand, and Communicate.* New York: Ballantine, 2001.

♪ Music for Young Children

Appleby, Amy, and Peter Pickow, eds. *The Library of Children's Song Classics.* New York: Amsco, 1993.

Bradford, Louise L., Ed. *Sing It Yourself: 220 Pentatonic American Folk Songs.* Sherman Oaks, CA: Alfred Publishing, 1978.

Brown, Marc. *Hand Rhymes.* New York: Penguin, 1985.

Campbell, Don. *The Mozart Effect for Children: Awakening Your Child's Mind, Health, and Creativity with Music.* New York: HarperCollins, 2000.

Cole, William, ed. *Folk Songs of England, Ireland, Scotland, and Wales.* Garden City, NY: Doubleday, 1961.

Cromie, William J. "Mozart Effect Hits Sour Note." *Harvard University Gazette,* September 16, 1999. http://www.news.harvard.edu/gazette/1999/09.16/mozart.html.

Daniel, Mark. *A Child's Treasury of Poems.* New York: Dial, 1986.

Feieraband, John M. *The Book of Songs and Rhymes with Beat Motions: Let's Clap Our Hands Together.* Chicago: GIA Publications, 2004.

_____. *The Book of Wiggles and Tickles.* Chicago: GIA Steps, 2000.

Fox, Dan. *A Treasury of Children's Songs: Forty Favorites to Sing and Play.* New York: Henry Holt, 2003.

_____. *Go In and Out the Window: An Illustrated Songbook for Young People.* New York: Metropolitan Museum of Art: Henry Holt, 1987.

Fuller, Cheri. *How to Grow a Young Music Lover.* Colorado Springs: Waterbrook Press, 2002.

Glazer, Tom. *Music for Ones and Twos: Songs and Games for the Very Young Child.* New York: Doubleday, 1983.

Hale, Glorya. *An Illustrated Treasury of Read-Aloud Poems for Young People.* New York: Black Dog and Leventhal, 2003.

Hansen, Dee, Elaine Bernstorf and Gayle M. Stuber. *The Music and Literacy Connection.* Reston, VA: The National Association for Music Education, 2004.

Kleiner, Lynn. *Toddlers Make Music! Ones and Twos! For Parents and Their Toddlers.* Van Nuys, CA: Alfred Publishing 2000.

Langstaff, Nancy, and John Langstaff, eds. *Jim Along, Josie: A Collection of Folk Songs and Singing Games for Young Children.* New York: Harcourt Brace Jovanovich, 1970.

Lomax, John, and Alan Lomax, eds. *Best-Loved American Folk Songs.* New York: Grosset and Dunlap, 1947.

_____. *Our Singing Country: Folk Songs and Ballads.* New York: Dover, 1941.

Orff-Schulwerk (American Edition). Volume 1. *Music for Children: Preschool.* Ed. Hermann Regner. Miami, FL: Schott Music, 1982.

Ortiz, John. *Nurturing Your Child with Music: How Sound Awareness Creates Happy, Smart, and Confident Children.* Hillsboro, OR: Beyond Words, 1999.

Piazza, Carolyn L. *Multiple Forms of Literacy: Teaching Literacy and the Arts.* Upper Saddle River, NJ: Prentice-Hall, 1999.

Rauscher, Frances H., Gordon L. Shaw, Linda J. Levine, and Katherine N. Ky. "Music and Spatial Task Performance: A Causal Relationship." Paper presented at the American Psychological Association 102nd Annual Convention, Los Angeles, California, 1994.

_____. "What Educators Must Learn from Science: The Case for Music in the Schools." In *Voice,* October 1995. www.wmea.org.

Sanders, Scott. *Hear the Wind Blow: American Folk Songs Retold.* New York: Bradbury Press, 1985.

Sandburg, Carl, ed. *The American Songbag.* New York: Harcourt, Brace, and World, 1927.

Seeger, Ruth Crawford, ed. *American Folk Songs for Children.* New York: Doubleday, 1948.

_____. *Animal Folk Songs for Children.* Hamden, CT: Linnet Books, 1950.

Sharp, Cecil J. and Maud Karpeles, Ed. *Folk Songs of the Southern Appalachians.* New York: Oxford University Press, 1932.

Simon, William L., ed. *The Reader's Digest Children's Songbook.* Pleasantville, NY: Reader's Digest Association, 1985.

Spergler, Kenneth. *The Bear: An American Folk Song.* New York: Mondo Publishing, 2002.

Standley, Jayne, "The Power of Contingent Music for Infant Learning." *Bulletin of the Council for Research in Music Education* 147 (Spring 2001), 65–85.

The National Association for Music Education. *The School Music Program: A New Vision.* http://www.menc.org/publication/books/prek12st.html.

Trehub, Sandra E. "Musical Predispositions in Infancy." In *Annals of the New York Academy of Sciences* 930 (June 2001):1–16.

Winn, Marie, ed. *The Fireside Book of Children's Songs.* New York: Simon and Schuster, 1966.

 Web Sites

ABC Teach
http://www.abcteach.com/index.html
Free and fee-based content, including downloads of seasonal craft ideas and learning games.

American Baby
http://www.americanbaby.com
From the popular parenting magazine, information on parenting topics.

American Sign Language Browser
http://commtechlab.msu.edu/sites/aslweb/browser.htm
This site provides hundreds of one-word video clips and instruction of ASL signs.

ASL PRO
http://aslpro.com
A video dictionary featuring conversational phrases, frequently used religious words, ASL for babies, and finger spelling quizzes.

Baby Center
http://www.babycenter.com
A site with a wide variety of resources on nearly every parenting topic from conception through childhood; also sells a range of products.

Baby Signs
http://www.babysigns.com
The official site for Acredolo and Goodwyn's Baby Signs program.

A Basic Dictionary of ASL Terms
http://www.masterstech-home.com/ASLDict.html
A sign dictionary that features the videos from the Michigan State University Web site (along with additional signs) and descriptions of the signs to aid in memory.

Becky Bailey's Loving Guidance and Conscious Discipline Programs
http://www.beckybailey.com
Information about the programs and products of Becky A. Bailey, Ph.D., the founder of Loving Guidance, Inc., a company dedicated to creating positive environments for children, families, schools, and businesses. Bailey is also the developer of the Conscious Discipline program.

Berkeley Parents Network
http://parents.berkeley.edu/advice/babies/signing.html
A forum for parents to offer advice and comments about their experiences with baby sign.

Brain Connection

http://www.brainconnection.com

An online source of information about the brain for educators, parents, students, and teachers.

Creative Homemaking

http://www.creativehomemaking.com/cooking/Feeding_Baby.shtml

Rachel Paxton, author of What's For Dinner?, *provides loads of practical advice including cleaning hints, organizing tips, gardening, home decorating, frugal living, holidays, crafts, and message forums. She has a great page featuring recipes and tips for feeding babies and toddlers.*

Do 2 Learn

http://www.do2learn.org

Line drawings to use for picture schedules and important tasks like using the bathroom and washing hands.

Handspeak

http://www.handspeak.com

Information about baby signs is included at this site for learning visual languages.

The Happiest Baby

http://www.thehappiestbaby.com/default.asp

Dr. Harvey Karp is a nationally renowned expert on children's health and the environment. His Web site shares information about his techniques for living with and loving babies and toddlers, as well as information about his books and classes.

Keep Kids Healthy

http://www.keepkidshealthy.com

A pediatrician-designed Web site offering free parenting advice, online forums, information regarding product recalls, and pediatric news updated daily.

Kids' Growth

http://www.kidsgrowth.com

A Web site tailored toward the concerns and interests of today's parents. The site was developed and created by well-respected medical leaders in the field of pediatrics and adolescent medicine. Members of the Medical Advisory Board oversee all Kids' Growth content, thereby guaranteeing its medical accuracy.

Kinder Signs: Baby Sign Language University

http://www.kindersigns.com

An Orlando, Florida–based program founded by speech pathologist Diane Ryan devoted to teaching parents how to communicate with their babies before they can speak.

Love Language

http://www.lovelanguageforbabies.com or http://www.babysingandsign.com

The official Web site for Baby Sing & Sign and the Kansas City–based Love Language program. Information about research, classes, and instructional products, as well as articles on getting started signing with babies. Song samples also available here.

Medline Plus

http://www.nlm.nih.gov/medlineplus/infantandtoddlerdevelopment.html

Sponsored by the National Library of Medicine and the National Institutes of Health, this site provides links to articles and other sites on a wide variety of health, development, and general parenting information.

Miss Jackie Music Company

http://www.jackiesilberg.com

Early childhood books and music for infants, toddlers, preschoolers and kindergartners from Jackie Silberg, better known as "Miss Jackie." Silberg is an internationally recognized authority on child development, a music educator, and a creator of games and activities that explore the nonsinging elements of music—sound, rhythm, language, movement, and instruments.

My Baby Can Talk

http://www.mybabycantalk.com

Features information about signing with babies and children, as well as a nicely done video dictionary including hundreds of words frequently used with babies and toddlers.

National Institute of Environmental Health Sciences (NIEHS) Kids' Pages

http://www.niehs.nih.gov/kids

A wonderful collection of resources for parents and educators, including an index with lyrics for hundreds of children's' songs. Many include a simple instrumental arrangement to help you learn or recall the melody.

Parenting

http://www.parenting.org

Short, practical articles on a number of parenting topics for babies through adolescents.

Peggy Seeger

www.pegseeger.com

Stories, humor, and information by Ms. Seeger about her experiences as a songwriter, singer, and member of the famous folksinging Seeger family. Family recordings from the Seeger family (Rounder Records) containing music collected by Ruth Crawford Seeger are also available here, including: American Folk Songs for Children, Animal Folk Songs for Children, *and* American Folk Songs for Christmas.

Public Broadcasting System

http://www.pbs.org/parents

Lots of information about parenting topics as well as information about their educational programming.

Sign 2 Me

http://www.sign2me.com

Information about Joseph Garcia's "Sign with Your Baby" program.

Wholesome Toddler Food

http://www.wholesometoddlerfood.com

Healthy, nutritious, and wholesome recipes, meals, and foods for your toddler are found at this site.

ABOUT THE AUTHOR

ANNE MEEKER MILLER, Ph.D., is the founder of the Love Language program. Through her writing and workshops, she shares information about the benefits of music, sign language, and play for infants and toddlers and gives easy and practical strategies for integrating all three into the daily lives of families.

Anne is a music therapist for the early childhood special education program of the Blue Valley School District in Overland Park, Kansas. Her preschool students were the inspiration for her work with sign language and music. Anne observed the way song and sign positively affected the language skills of her students, and she wanted to have an even earlier influence in the lives of children, when language is first acquired.

Anne has taught music to students from preschool through college levels. She received the Excellence in Teaching award given by the Learning Exchange, Kansas City Chamber of Commerce, and the *Kansas City Star*. She was a commission member of the Housewright Symposium on the Future of Music Education sponsored by the Music Educators National Conference. She is a featured columnist for the parenting magazine *Mother and Child Reunion*.

She is the author of *Baby Sing & Sign: Communicate Early with Your Baby—Learning Signs the Fun Way through Music and Play* and *Toddler Sing & Sign: Improve Your Child's Vocabulary and Verbal Skills the Fun Way—Through Music and Play*. A composer and folk musician, Miller performs her music in the Kansas City area. Her debut album, *Bright-Eyed and Bushy-Tailed,* won NAPPA and Parent's Choice Honors awards.

Anne lives in Olathe, Kansas, where she enjoys spending time with her husband, three sons, and wheaten terrier. Her hobbies include laundry and carpooling.

CONTRIBUTORS

♪ Jennifer Ferguson

Jennifer was a special education preschool teacher for ten years with the Blue Valley School District in Overland Park, Kansas, where she worked with typically developing young children and children with special needs. While in Blue Valley, she received the Fox 4 News Crystal Apple Award and the Excellence in Education Award for her teaching contributions, and served on the State of Kansas Standards Development Committee to assist in the development of Kansas Early Learning Guidelines. She is currently the *Baby Sing & Sign* National Training Director and teaches classes at two major medical centers in the Kansas City area. Jennifer attended the University of Kansas for her undergraduate and graduate studies. She has a bachelor's degree in Speech Pathology and Audiology and dual master's degrees in Early Childhood Special Education and Early Childhood Deaf Education. Throughout her teaching experiences, Jennifer has consistently used sign language, music, and movement to enhance communication and learning. She is continuing that mission through her teaching and training of *Baby Sing & Sign*.

Jennifer lives in Leawood, Kansas, with her husband, Aaron, toddler, Maizie, and miniature dachshund, Izzy. She created the sign language definitions as well as the "Play, Sign, and Learn" pieces and picture book suggestions for the book.

♪ Amy Martin, Photographer

After a previous life as a computer software designer and several wonderful years at home raising her three beautiful daughters, Amy Martin decided to follow her passion and began a new career as a portrait photographer. With the encouragement and support of her family and friends, she started a small studio in the Kansas City area, where she spends her time capturing the magic and innocence of small children. Amy's work was also featured in Anne Meeker Miller's *Baby Sing & Sign* and *Toddler Sing & Sign* books.

Amy lives in Olathe, Kansas, with her über-hottie husband, daughters, Katie, Abigail, and Elizabeth, and a small menagerie of four-legged friends. Her photographs are a favorite feature of Miller's *Sing & Sign* books and capture the playfulness and fun we aspire to share with our readers.

♪ Cindy Daugherty, M.D., Consultant

Cindy Daugherty, M.D., is a practicing pediatrician and mother of three. She is certified by the American Board of Pediatrics and is a Fellow of the American Academy of Pediatrics. She is the co-founder of After-Hours Pediatrics, a kids-only acute care clinic in Overland Park, Kansas. She enjoys signing with patients.

♪ Christina Stewart, Consultant

Christina Stewart earned a Bachelor of Science in Dietetics from the University of Nebraska-Kearney and a Master of Science in Nutrition from the University of Cincinnati. She currently works as a pediatric clinical nutrition specialist for a children's hospital in the Kansas City area. Christina enjoys singing and signing with her two sons, Jackson and Alexander.

♪ Ingrid Bullard, Consultant

Ingrid Bullard is a speech and language pathologist. She earned her B.A. from the University of South Florida in Communication Sciences and Disorders in 1999 and Masters in Speech Language Pathology in May of 2002. She completed her Clinical Fellowship in December of 2005. She lives in Florida with her husband and young daughter.

ACKNOWLEDGMENTS

THANK YOU without end to Jennifer Bourne Ferguson, my right and left hands, for writing, reading, listening, organizing, analyzing, clarifying, empathizing, and "humorizing" with me in appropriate measure 24/7. Thanks to Maizie for being our inspiration.

Bravo to my focus group; you are the heart of this project. I can never thank you enough for loving and nourishing this "baby" with all of your good ideas, advice, and stories: Darcy Beaver, Jill Beveridge, Ingrid Bullard, Julie Crainshaw, Wendee Egbert, Jonann Ellner, Tonya Gast, Channy Gotfredson, Kelly Hill, Carri Kasick, Missie Klusman, Gwen Landever, Kelly Lawson, Zoe Miller, Karla Pahl, Chrissy Stewart, Myra Valdez, Carol Webster, and Angela Windsor. Special thanks to my "e-mail editors," Melinda Young and Kelly Hill; to Collette Barnes-Maelzer and Robin Olson for guiding my signing hands; and to wise and wonderful Carol Webster for her preface. I am grateful to Jeff Petrie for his fabulous graphic art.

Thanks to all of those whose photographs appear in the book: Dale Bourne, Brook Bullard, Avery Burr, Tabitha Burt, Rowan Khai Carrico, Madeline Carter, Jack Clayton, Lauren Deel, Alyssa Egbert, Zac Ellner, Aaron Ferguson, Maizie Ferguson, David Gast, Ellie Gast, Gabe Gast, Gilli Gerson, Rosie Hankins, Aidan Hayes, Ethan Inks, Max Kasick, Jill Klusman, Sofia Loveland, Stephanie Meyer, Tate Meyer, Augusta Anne Miller, Isabella Miller, Chloe Nix, Faith Parker, Jonathan Patnode, Henry Schulewitz, Marissa Schoenhals, Matan Siegel, Blake Smith, Trace Taylor, Adelina Valdez, Skyler Vince, Ava Vondemkamp, and Reece Widman.

Hooray for my sign language "super" models: Erin Burge, Jennifer Ferguson, John Hansen, and Sheryl Porter. Elle McPherson's got nothin' on you. A special shout-out to Darcy Beaver, Cindy Giddings, Pola Firestone, and Kelly Werts, the original "birth parents" of *Baby Sing & Sign*.

Thanks to vocalists Hayden, Riley, and Tyler Anne Burch; Steve, Courtney, Logan, Grant and Ivy Flynn Daugherty; Kevin Hazelton, Adam Holthus, Greg and Andy Miller, and Nicole McCroskey, Josh Young; jazz pianist Chris Hazelton; drummer Mike Nicholis; and the members of Konza Swamp: Jimmy Campbell, slide guitar; Chris DeVictor, bass; Caleb Gardner, mandolin; Nick Gardner, banjo; Beth Watts, vocals and guitar; Garrett White, vocals and guitar; and the group Quadio: Grant Hunget, Rob Mathieu, Matt Moore, and Michael Troyer. Thank you, Jan Holthus, for creating the musical scores. And the biggest "high five" of all to Richard McCroskey and Rick Burch for the musical delicacies you two have dished out. You are amazing.

Affection and appreciation to my favorite cowboy and literary agent, Neil Salkind, for getting this show on the road, and to Courtney Napoles, my brilliant editor, who used her magic powers for good on my manuscript and made this book much better. Effusive thanks to Amy Martin, Photographer Emeritus, for her wonderful photographs and diving headfirst into these books.

I would be remiss if I did not thank the following for their integral involvement in this project: Renee Caputo, Barb and Tony, Lindt truffles, my Other Mother, the Sassies, UB and Pam, iPod, Cooper, the Herms, Carri and Sparks, Dr. Kinks, Twila, Jane, Tostitos with just a hint of lime, Clorox All-Fabric Bleach, Mrs. Dr. Dunn, Emily Wagner, Judi, all of New York City, Four Joy, every paraprofessional I have ever worked with, Julie and Brian, my sister Nancy, Chipotle, Dad and Bette, Elphaba, Oprah, Alice-Ann, Kendall and Amy, the Cosgrove Family Singers, Marcheta and Pam, Mary and Terry, the Jayhawk, Peggy and Irene, Ralph, Costco, the KIDZ Committee, Diet Dr. Pepper, Mrs. Burch, Eva Cassidy, Nurses Terry and Denise, Joy, Chris and Caroline, Ermil, Ruth Crawford Seeger, "Doncha," Nanette, Keith Urban, my heavenly angel mama, pajama pants with elastic waistbands, the amazing Donna Lynn, Starbucks, God, my nearly-saint-like husband, Dan, and my fine fiddlers three, "Mr. McGreggor," "Kev," and "Bear."

And lastly, thank you to all the families, caregivers, teachers, and therapists I have met across the country and back home in my classes at Shawnee Mission Medical Center and the Blue Valley School District. "Because I knew you, I have been changed for good."

—AMM

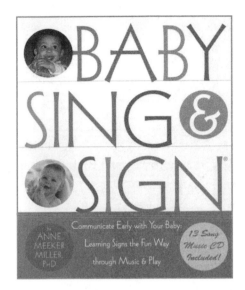

MEALTIME & BEDTIME SING & SIGN

MUSIC CD

1. MY KITCHEN DOOR
2. CRAWLY, CREEPY LITTLE MOUSIE
3. THE MUFFIN MAN
4. FILL THE BASKET
5. JOHN THE RABBIT
6. WHAT DID YOU HAVE FOR YOUR SUPPER?
7. MISTER MOON
8. WE'RE HAVING A BATH
9. WHITE SHEEP AND BLACK SHEEP
10. WHAT'LL WE DO WITH THE BABY?
11. RAINBOWS, RAILROADS, AND RHYMES
12. NOW I LAY ME DOWN TO SLEEP

Produced by Anne Meeker Miller and Rick Burch.
Engineered and Mixed by Rick Burch/KC Creative Media
Mastered by Richard McCroskey